Western Profiles of Innovative Agricultural Marketing
Examples from Direct Farm Marketing and Agri-Tourism Enterprises

 Western Extension Marketing Committee

Western Extension Marketing Committee Authors

Russell Tronstad (Managing Editor), University of Arizona

DeeVon Bailey, Utah State University
Larry Lev, Oregon State University
Ramiro Lobo, University of California, Davis
Stuart T. Nakamoto, University of Hawaii
Wendy Umberger, Colorado State University
Ruby Ward, Utah State University

Other Contributing Authors

Kent Fleming, University of Hawaii
Dean Miner, Utah State University
William Riggs, University of Nevada, Reno
Rod Sharp, Colorado State University
Etaferahu Takele, University of California, Davis
Dawn Thilmany, Colorado State University

Editing, Layout, and Design

Nancy Bannister, University of Arizona

Sponsors

Western Center for Risk Management Education
USDA Risk Management Agency
Farm Foundation

Western Profiles of Innovative Agricultural Marketing:
Examples from Direct Farm Marketing and Agri-Tourism Enterprises

Published 2003 by the Western Extension Marketing Committee

©2003 All rights reserved by authors

ISBN: 0-9748669-0-3

Photo Credits:

Covers
Ramiro Lobo (large photo); Honeyacre Enterprises Ltd.;
Dean Miner; Russell Tronstad; Stuart T. Nakamoto;
William Riggs; Ken Love; Rod Sharp

Introduction
Ramiro Lobo

Creative Growers
Gary Stephenson

Seabreeze Organic Farm
Ramiro Lobo

Nalo Farms
Stuart T. Nakamoto

Love Family Farms
Ken Love

Cattail Creek Farm
Oregon State University Extension
and Experiment Station Communication

Rocky Mountain Beef Cooperative
Rod Sharp

The Holualoa Kona Coffee Company
Stuart T. Nakamoto

Sunfresh Farms
Russell Tronstad

English Farm
Rod Sharp

Schnepf Farms
Russell Tronstad

Mother Nature's Farm
Russell Tronstad

Southridge Farms
Dean Miner

Mebane Farms
Rod Sharp

Honeyacre Produce Company
Honeyacre Enterprises Ltd.

American Pet Diner
William Riggs

Thompson Farms
The Food Alliance

Harward Farms
Dean Miner

Summary
Ramiro Lobo

Issued in furtherance of Cooperative Extension work, acts of May 8 and June 30, 1914, in cooperation with the U.S. Department of Agriculture, James A. Christenson, Director, Cooperative Extension, College of Agriculture and Life Sciences, The University of Arizona.

The University of Arizona is an equal opportunity, affirmative action institution. The University does not discriminate on the basis of race, color, religion, sex, national origin, age, disability, veteran status, or sexual orientation in its programs and activities.

Contents

v | **Preface**
Russell Tronstad

1 | **Introduction:** Getting Started with Direct Farm Marketing and Agri-Tourism
Rod Sharp and William Riggs

7 | **Creative Growers:** Pursuing a "Customer Intimacy" Approach
Larry Lev

13 | **Seabreeze Organic Farm:** Farming on the Urban Edge
Ramiro Lobo and Etaferahu Takele

21 | **Nalo Farms:** Servicing High-End Restaurants
Stuart T. Nakamoto

27 | **Love Family Farms:** Kona Coffee for the Japanese Market
Kent Fleming and Stuart T. Nakamoto

35 | **Cattail Creek Farm:** Building a Successful Part-Time Farm through Informal Collaborative Agreements
Larry Lev

41 | **Rocky Mountain Beef Cooperative:** Marketing "Natural" Beef
Rod Sharp

47 | **The Holualoa Kona Coffee Company:** Marketing Memorable Experiences and High-Quality Products
Stuart T. Nakamoto and Kent Fleming

55 | **Sunfresh Farms:** A Project That Quickly Mushroomed into a Large Direct-Marketing Business
Russell Tronstad

63 | **English Farm:** Krazy Korn Maze
Rod Sharp

67 | **Schnepf Farms:** The Southwest's Premier Family Entertainment Farm
Russell Tronstad

75 | **Mother Nature's Farm:** Marketing the Farm Experience and Diverse Products
Russell Tronstad

83 | **Southridge Farms:** Moose Droppings for Sale
Ruby Ward, DeeVon Bailey, and Dean Miner

89 | **Mebane Farms:** Pastured Poultry
Rod Sharp

93 | **Honeyacre Produce Company:** Successfully Adapting to Change
Wendy Umberger and Dawn Thilmany

101 | **American Pet Diner:** Marketing Alfalfa to Pets
William Riggs

107 | **Thompson Farms:** Do Real Farmers Sell Direct?
Larry Lev

113 | **Harward Farms:** Sweet Corn
Ruby Ward, DeeVon Bailey, and Dean Miner

119 | **Summary:** Guiding Principles for Innovative Direct Marketing of Agricultural Products
Wendy Umberger, Larry Lev, and Russell Tronstad

Copies of this publication are available for purchase through the University of Arizona College of Agriculture and Life Science's publications system. Please visit **http://cals.arizona.edu/pubs/** or write to the following address:

>CALSmart
>4042 N. Campbell Avenue
>Tucson, AZ 85719-1111
>Phone: (520) 318-7275
>Fax: (520) 795-8508
>Toll free: 1-877-763-5315

In addition, you may freely download and print copies of the book from the Western Extension Marketing Committee site: **http://cals.arizona.edu/arec/wemc/westernprofiles.html**

Preface

In recent years, traditional commodity marketing channels have not provided sufficient returns for many small- and medium-sized farmers to maintain a viable livelihood through only farm activities. This publication examines how several operations in the West have migrated from a traditional commodity-focused business into a successful direct-marketing enterprise within the last 10 to 15 years. Declining profit margins that would not sustain their families' livelihood on the farm was the main reason that prompted these operations to consider direct-marketing and agri-tourism activities.

Even though direct marketing allows farmers to retain a much higher share of consumer food expenditures, the elements needed to make this production-marketing strategy a success are often not well understood. In part, this is because of their increased complexity as compared to commodity production-marketing systems. Albert Einstein's famous quotation that "Not everything that can be counted counts, and not everything that counts can be counted," may seem all too appropriate when looking at what it takes to thrive at direct farm marketing and agri-tourism. Traditionally, commodity producers have set goals for high yields and low costs of production in order to be "low cost" producers. However, personality skills, relationships, superb quality and service, willingness to change, and general business savvy were also found to be key for the direct farm marketing and agri-tourism enterprises examined. This book is not intended to be a step-by-step guide on how to start a direct farm marketing or agri-tourism enterprise, but rather to identify the more subtle and unique factors behind the failures and successes of the enterprises examined and to determine their strategies for meeting future challenges and risks.

This publication examines 17 direct farm marketing and agri-tourism enterprises from the West and also includes introductory and summary sections. The end of each section provides contact information for the enterprises examined and for the contributing authors. The Western Extension Marketing Committee is greatly indebted to the willingness and openness of all interviewed participants to share the strategies, successes, and failures of their enterprises and what their plans are for meeting future challenges and risks.

A special thanks and acknowledgment is given to Nancy Bannister for her dedication and superb work in the technical editing, layout, and design of this publication. She did a great job of bringing consistency to the terms and writing style of 13 different authors and was persistent in getting photos that would fit the text and look attractive. Thanks are also due Joanne Littlefield for videotaping interviews of Arizona's enterprises. Finally, the Western Extension Marketing Committee would like to thank the Farm Foundation for seed money that started this project and the Western Center for Risk Management Education and USDA Risk Management Agency for providing the primary financial support that made *Western Profiles of Innovative Agricultural Marketing* possible.

—*Russell Tronstad*

Introduction

Getting Started with Direct Farm Marketing and Agri-Tourism

Rod Sharp and William Riggs

Direct farm marketing is the process of selling a product or service directly to the consumer. It allows the producer to capture a larger share of the consumer's dollar, reach new markets, and/or establish a unique identity. As described in the figure on page 2, the overall value added by farmers and ranchers of consumer food expenditures has fallen from 22.8 percent in 1950 to only 7.9 percent in 2000. The figure that follows on page 3 shows that total food expenditures in 2000 dollars have more than doubled from 1950 to 2000, increasing at about 1.4 percent annually. However, total farm value and value added by farmers has declined slightly over this period. This decline has occurred even though the quantity of raw commodities produced, such as corn, soybeans, and wheat, has increased by 259 percent, 822 percent, and 119 percent. Clearly, producing more output does not equate with higher profit margins or even higher gross sales. This publication is intended to help producers identify avenues for providing more value to consumers at the farm or ranch level.

But in order to use direct marketing or agri-tourism as a vehicle to increase profitability, a clear understanding is needed of production costs and of consumers' tastes and desires. This requires a different set of management and personality skills from what traditional commodity-focused operations have used and not all individuals are suited to make this transition. Direct farm marketing and agri-tourism enterprises require more people skills, management, investment, and time than traditional commodity-focused farms. Before starting a direct-marketing or agri-tourism venture, proper business research and planning must be made or else the venture will most likely fail. In addition to examining the economic viability of the business, an assessment must be made of management skills, personal qualities, family needs, and lifestyle preferences.

To be successful, the venture must have a targeted product mix and quality that is attractive to consumers, must show growth potential, and must generate a cash flow that is solvent for the short term and profitable to grow over time. The venture should also fit with any business and community goals established since local consumers are often the strongest supporters of direct-marketing and agri-tourism operations.

Introduction: Getting Started with Direct Farm Marketing and Agri-Tourism

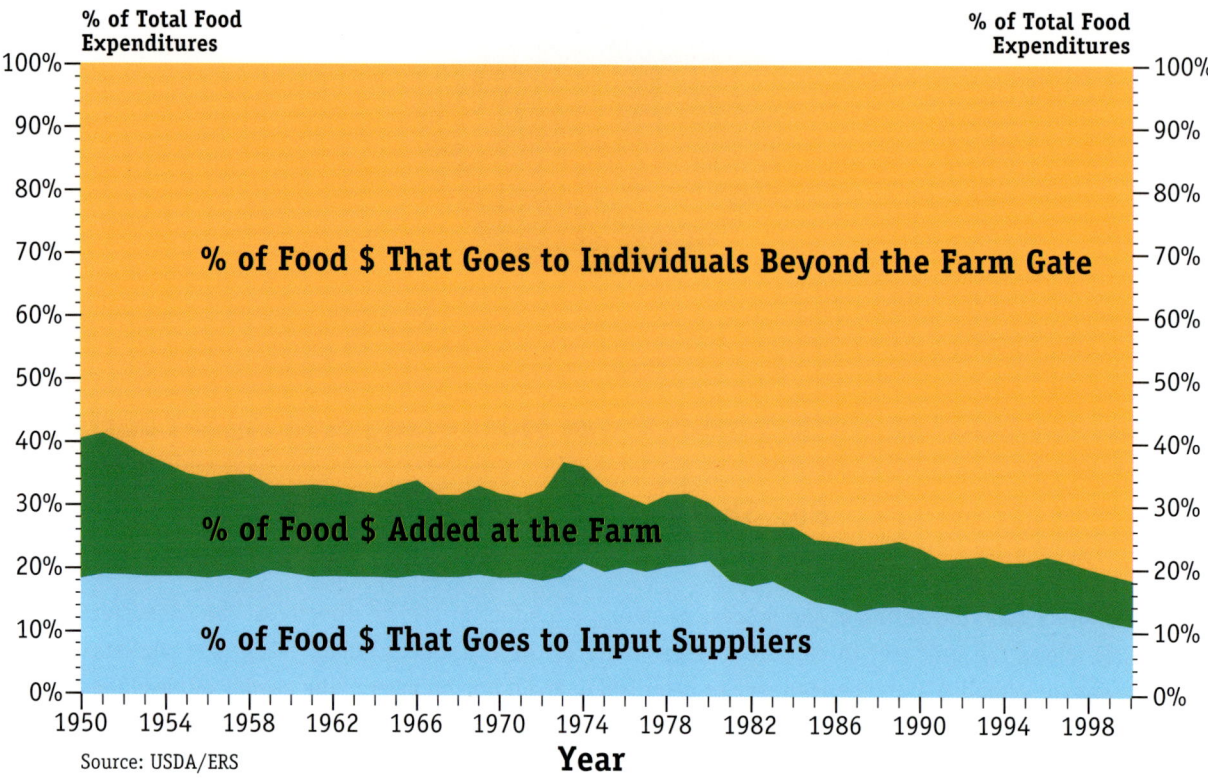

Source: USDA/ERS

Getting Started

Planning is an essential ingredient for any successful business. A detailed business plan should be written that demonstrates the products and services proposed can be sold at a profit over the long run and also meet short-term cash flow requirements.

The three primary reasons for writing business plans are to (1) aid in determining the feasibility of a business idea, (2) attract capital for start-up and operation, and (3) provide direction for future potential growth after it is in operation. A good plan gives the reader information on "the what, when, where, why, and how" the business will accomplish its objectives and who will be involved.

A plan's contents will vary from business to business; however, its structure is fairly standardized. Your plan should contain as many of the following sections as appropriate for your type of venture.

1. **Cover Page**
   Include names, titles, and contact information associated with the business.

2. **Table of Contents**
   An orderly table of contents will allow the reader to turn directly to the section desired.

3. **Executive Summary**
   A one- to two-page overview of your business plan is likely the most important section since most financial lenders and potential business partners will not need to read beyond this summary if it is well written.

Components of Food Expenditures, 1950–2000

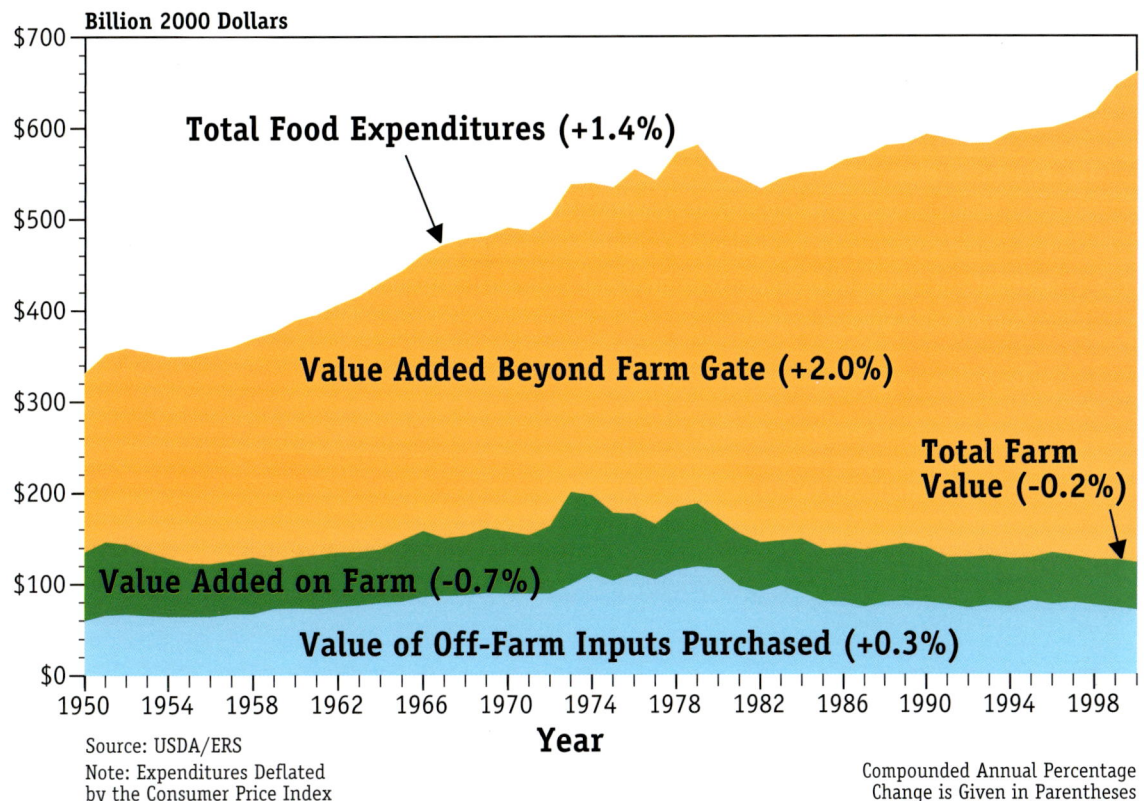

Source: USDA/ERS
Note: Expenditures Deflated by the Consumer Price Index
Compounded Annual Percentage Change is Given in Parentheses

4. **Company and Industry Background Information**
   Describe your company background, legal needs, personal skills, previous experience, financial resources, environment, and industry trends.

5. **Description of Products or Services**
   Go into detail describing your products or services. Describe your competitive advantage and what sets your products or services apart as better than the competition's.

6. **Marketing Plan**
   The marketing plan shows how you expect to reach your sales forecast. Include an overall market strategy, market objectives, pricing policy, promotion policy, and place and service policies.

7. **Operations Plan**
   The operations plan will stress elements related to your business production. Include facilities, location, capital equipment, labor force, inventory, and purchasing.

8. **Management Team**
   Describe the legal form of ownership and the people with their qualifications that will make the business run smoothly and successfully.

9. **Timeline**
   Outline the interrelationship and timing of the major events planned for your venture.

10. Critical Risks and Assumptions

All business plans contain implicit assumptions. This section gives you a place to establish alternative plans in case the unexpected happens (unreliable sales forecasts, erratic supply of products or raw materials, etc.).

11. Community Impacts

Describe the potential benefits, networks, and alliances with the community.

12. Financial Plan

Your financial plan is where you demonstrate that all the information from previous sections can come together to form a viable, profitable business. Projections should be your best estimate of future operations. Your financial plan should include the following statements:

- Sources and uses of capital,
- Cash flow projections for three years,
- Balance sheets for three years,
- Income statements for three years, and
- Financial analysis (liquidity, solvency, financial efficiency, profitability, repayment capacity, and break-even analysis).

Where to Get Help

The business plan should be tailored to fit the direct-marketing project. Write the plan yourself, even if you seek assistance from professionals and other community members. Professional assistance (attorneys, accountants, financial consultants, etc.) should be used as needed.

There are several resources available to assist in writing a business plan. Listed below are just a few to get you started:

- Small Business Administration
  1-800-827-5722
  www.sba.gov

- Small Business Development Centers
  www.sba.gov/sbdc/

- Chambers of Commerce
  www.acce.org

- Colleges and Universities

- State Economic Development Agencies

- Libraries

- Business Information Centers (BICs)
  www.sba.gov/BI/bics/index.html

- National Sustainable Agriculture Education Service
  attra.ncat.org/

- *The Legal Guide for Direct Farm Marketing* by Neil Hamilton
  www.statefoodpolicy.org/legal_guide.htm

- *Direct Farm Marketing and Tourism Handbook* (available for download)
  ag.arizona.edu/arec/pubs/dmkt/dmkt.html

Keys to Success

The Southern Sustainable Agriculture Working Group and The National Center for Appropriate Technology interviewed successful farmers to determine what they learned in marketing directly to consumers. A few general practices emerged that could be considered as "Keys to Success."[1]

- ***Choose something you like (love) to do.***
  Most people start value-added activities to make more money. Your sincere enthusiasm and belief in your product are part of what make you unique. Without doing something you love to do, it is difficult to find the energy and motivation to stick with it.

- ***Provide quality.***
  Offer a high-quality product or service. High quality with some unique trait is an avenue that many direct marketers pursue to differentiate their product. Quality is made up of many dimensions (fresher, better tasting, healthier, more consistent, or cleaner product; thoughtful presentation or packaging/labeling, etc.). It may be tempting to use substandard inputs or service, but most direct marketers today find that a great experience or quality product is more important for attracting consumers than a low price. The consumer knows value and if you're shooting for low quality and price, direct marketers can seldom compete with large wholesale and retail outlets.

- ***Start small and grow naturally.***
  Starting small usually means investing less money and borrowing less. Starting small also means mistakes are less costly; remember, it is easier to manage a small operation.

- ***Keep good records (production, financial, regulatory).***
  Trying to manage without good information is like trying to find an address without a map. Good information and records are necessary for knowing whether or not you are meeting your goals and for understanding reasons why your goals are or are not being met.

- ***Provide what the consumer/customer wants.***
  There are two approaches to agricultural marketing: "push" and "pull." The push approach implies producing a product and then pushing it onto consumers for the going market price—the traditional way of marketing many commodity crops. The pull strategy, however, is increasingly becoming the norm in today's environment. Under this approach, specific products and desired product attributes are targeted using consumer preferences so that the seller is not entirely a price taker at the market place.

- ***Maintain a loyal (preferably local) customer base.***
  An important way to capitalize on your uniqueness is through relationship marketing. You are unique and no one can do exactly what you can do. These personal relationships and the trust

---

[1] Born, Holly. *Keys to Success in Value-Added Agriculture.* Southern Sustainable Agriculture Working Group and the National Center for Appropriate Technology's ATTRA Project. 2001.

they engender over time are effective marketing strategies. Local customers are generally the easiest to develop into a solid, loyal customer base.

- ***Provide more than just a product.***
  Most successful value-added businesses provide more than just a product or service. They provide an experience that can be in the form of pleasant social interactions, a chance to experience the rural way of life, education, services, tours, etc.

- ***Involve others.***
  Get the whole family, partners, and/or community involved. Take advantage of different skills and talents.

- ***Keep informed.***
  You must keep informed on every aspect concerning your business, consumer wants, competition, finances, etc.

- ***Plan for the future.***
  Fail to plan and you plan to fail. It's true. Planning is essential to success. In planning be realistic in terms of goals, pricing, costs, time commitments, etc. Be flexible and realize that the best-laid plans can go wrong and that things change.

- ***Evaluate continually.***
  Things are always changing. You need to constantly monitor and evaluate what is going on in your business. It is impossible to know if you are reaching your goals without taking the time to evaluate.

- ***Persevere.***
  You need a good deal of perseverance just to figure out how to produce the products, much less how to market them. Identifying your niche and building a customer base takes time.

- ***Secure adequate capitalization.***
  A direct-marketing or agri-tourism business is likely to operate at a loss for at least the first year or more of operation. Make sure you have adequate liquid financial reserves to meet set-up costs and cash flow requirements. Many businesses fail because they did not secure enough capital to see their venture through to a positive cash flow.

Planning is important and the key to success for all types of business ventures, including direct marketing and agri-tourism. Before starting, be prepared. While much of the market risk of adverse price swings is removed with a direct-marketing enterprise, risks associated with production (quality and yield), events being rained out, greater labor skill requirements, and liability risks require that careful risk assessments are made before disaster strikes. Dr. Neil Hamilton's book of *The Legal Guide for Direct Farm Marketing* (Drake University Agricultural Law Center and USDA Sustainable Agriculture Research and Education [SARE]. 235 pp. June 1999) is a good resource for assessing the legal risks of a direct farm marketing or agri-tourism enterprise (www.statefoodpolicy.org/legal_guide.htm). Most ventures will fail without proper research and planning. Assess your management skills and personal qualities as well as your family needs and lifestyle preferences. With proper planning, you will position yourself to be successful.

Creative Growers

Pursuing a "Customer Intimacy" Approach

Larry Lev

The *Discipline of Market Leaders*, a book on business strategy, describes three alternative approaches that a business can follow toward success:[1]
- Operational Efficiency—producing at the lowest possible cost (McDonald's, Wal-Mart)
- Product Leadership—being first with new products (Intel, Nike)
- Customer Intimacy—meeting the specific needs of select customers (Nordstrom, Airborne Express)

In the United States, most agricultural producers follow the path of "operational efficiency" by producing commodities at the lowest possible cost. Aaron and Kelly Silverman, owners of Creative Growers, followed a different course. They chose the less traveled "customer intimacy" route. All of their farm enterprises provide high-quality products to specific customers. Their objective is to build a successful farm by filling certain niches in the local food system.

Creative Growers Farm produces three distinct sets of products and markets them through five different distribution channels. The farm is organized as follows:

1. Vegetable Production (63% of total revenues)
- Direct marketing of high-quality produce and herbs to restaurants (56%)—*the focus of this study*
- Weekly baskets of produce and herbs to a 15-member Community Supported Agriculture (CSA) program (7%)

2. Direct-marketing of pastured poultry (26%)

3. Flower Production (11%)
- Farmers' market sales of cut flowers (7%)
- Direct marketing of cut flowers to businesses (4%)

---

[1] Treacy, Michael and Fred Wiersema. *The Discipline of Market Leaders.* Cambridge Massachusetts: Perseus Books. 1995. [Now available from DIANE Publishing Company, Collingdale, PA. Sept. 2001.]

Creative Growers: Pursuing a "Customer Intimacy" Approach

The Silvermans live and farm in the small community of Noti, about 25 miles due west of Eugene, Oregon (population 130,000), their primary market. Aaron manages vegetable and poultry production while Kelly is responsible for flower production. Although the farm is moving towards a full-time, year-round operation, the Silvermans have subsidized it with off-farm income during their first four years. Their gross farm sales recently passed the $100,000 level.

Creative Growers Farm is small by most standards. Out of 22 owned acres, three are devoted to 30 different vegetable crops. Most of the remaining acres are in pasture and dedicated to the poultry enterprise. Five additional acres are rented from a neighbor and used for crop production. The Silvermans employ three people during the growing season. The business is growing slowly because Aaron wants to be sure his products meet the needs of his customers before he expands production.

Competitive Advantage

Creative Growers sells more than 30 different organically grown vegetables to a small group of restaurants in Eugene. Restaurant supply has always been a highly price-competitive market and this competition may continue to increase. For example, the Internet firm FOODgalaxy.com recruits suppliers and restaurants by promising to make the purchasing process more efficient. FOODgalaxy provides software that allows a restaurant to automatically split orders among suppliers based on the lowest price for individual items (see their website for additional information). Restaurants are promised reductions in costs through less time spent on ordering.

Aaron, in contrast, offers something quite different to his restaurant customers. Since 1996 (when he began farming), he has cultivated individual chefs by providing what the Creative Growers order sheet describes as "products that are of superior quality and require minimal preparation prior to use." To get started, Aaron targeted likely restaurants and made face-to-face contacts in order to sell both his products and himself. For each ongoing customer, Silverman carefully harvests the crops himself, takes each order to the restaurant kitchen, puts it away, and rotates stock in the process. In return for this high level of service and guaranteed quality, he charges full retail prices for his products instead of wholesale. Two keys to Creative Growers' financial viability are that he receives per-unit prices from commercial customers that are equal to or higher than what he could get for the same products at the local farmers' market and that each order is fairly substantial. As a result, Silverman can earn as much from five quick restaurant deliveries as others earn from devoting most of a day to the farmers' market.

> "When introducing a new crop, Silverman produces only a small amount to see how it goes."

How is he able to do this? "The chefs are more willing than even the best farmers' market customers to pay for the quality that I provide," Silverman explains. Even though Creative Growers receives top dollar for its vegetables, on a per-plate basis the cost of the vegetables represents a small percentage of what consumers pay.

The table shows a sample of the information Aaron provides to his customers.

Item	Projected Duration	Target Price
Arugula	Early April–End November	$7 per pound
Basil: green, purple, cinnamon, Thai, and lemon—loosely packed tips, no stem	Early June–End September	$9 per pound
Eggplant: baby Italian, Japanese	Mid-July–September Mid-July–September	$3 per pound $1.85 per pound

Although Silverman does not have formal contracts with the restaurants, he does have excellent communication with them. Over the winter, he sits down with each chef to plan production according to his or her needs. When introducing a new crop, he produces only a small amount to see how it goes, both in production and for his customers. He is committed to excellent quality *before* he makes the sale and will plow under a crop that does not meet his standards.

Silverman recognizes that he must have a broad selection of products to be of interest to restaurants as a regular supplier. He must also clearly understand the ebb and flow of each restaurant because he will lose sales if he misjudges products and quantities. During the season, he constantly tweaks production to provide what fits best with his clients' menus. While he prefers to grow crops that provide the best return (he maintains extremely detailed records), he is willing to produce certain crops for his restaurants as loss leaders. Silverman also provides the restaurants with a list of crops he cannot/will not grow so they can get them from other suppliers.

Perceived Threats

- **One or more of his major clients goes out of business.** Because Silverman's business is based on relationships and because the restaurant business is so volatile, this is a very real threat. It takes years to cultivate a good client, but he may lose that client overnight if the restaurant goes out of business or the chef leaves. To date neither has occurred, but he recognizes it as a major risk and addresses this threat by maintaining a diverse set of clients.

- **Insufficient or poor quality labor.** Although Creative Growers is a small business that does not hire a lot of help, the help that is hired must be of high quality. In one recent season, a Creative Growers employee was not maintaining the required quality standards and business suffered as a result. Aaron fired the worker and has been more careful ever since.

- **Inability to expand due to lack of access to the facilities of a neighboring farm.** Aaron has been able to use the facilities and equipment of a much larger neighboring farm. Losing that access would cause Silverman's business to suffer. Aaron has been working on increasing the capital stock of his farm through grant writing.

- **Economic downturn.** All of Aaron's products target wealthier customers and are higher-quality versions of "standard" products. If the economy were to turn sour, would people cut back on restaurant meals, free-range chickens, and flowers?

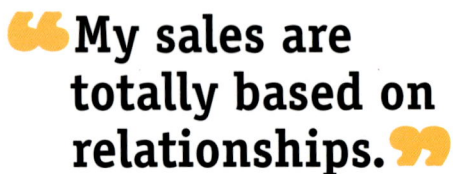

> "My sales are totally based on relationships."

Interestingly, two threats one might expect Creative Growers to face are not among those Silverman perceives. First, he does not feel someone else can steal his customers. "My sales are totally based on relationships. The chefs like me and they like my products. They will not simply switch to an alternate supplier because of price." So, Silverman does not feel direct competition from other local growers or distributors. Secondly, because he produces so many different crops, Silverman does not view weather as a major threat. In any given season, some crops flourish while others do not, but every year he will have successes.

Integrating Different Parts of the Farm into a System

One of the keys to Silverman's success is that he views his farm as a *system* and has a thorough understanding of how its individual enterprises fit together. So, while he is interested in the sales of each component, he is aware of the impact each has on the others and will reduce or eliminate an enterprise if it adversely affects the whole farm.

- The small CSA program provides additional cash flow and makes use of excess and sometimes lower-quality produce. Silverman does not plan to expand it.

- The two flower enterprises are semi-autonomous parts of the business, overseen by Kelly and with a separate clientele. Though Kelly sells flowers at the local farmers' market, she does not sell the farm's produce there. The Silvermans feel that would require hiring an additional salesperson and believe they can earn higher prices for their produce from their other outlets.

- The direct-marketed chickens represent a smaller supplemental enterprise that provides fertilizer for the rest of the farm and has the potential for substantial growth. In the early years, poultry represented as much as 65 percent of total income and in time this enterprise may again become the largest part of the farm. Expansion is limited by the lack of infrastructure (for inputs, slaughter, etc.). Looking ahead, if he can overcome regulatory hurdles, Silverman wants to integrate poultry sales into both the restaurant supply and farmers' market aspects of his business. He already provides chickens to his chefs to test quality, and he plans to conduct market surveys in a number of farmers' markets. To make his poultry venture work, he plans to form a cooperative with two farmers who use similar production techniques.

> **He views his farm as a *system* and has a thorough understanding of how its individual enterprises fit together.**

Market Research
Silverman carefully researches all of his markets and products before entering production. Once in production, he gradually increases his volume as he determines the new enterprise will fit into the overall farm. For example, he will conduct consumer research in farmers' markets before he markets his poultry products there.

Replicability
Someone with similar skills could copy each of the Creative Growers enterprises. But the individual niches are narrow enough in the Eugene area that Aaron believes entrants do not pose a big threat to his business. So, replication is more likely to take place in a different geographic area.

Key Points and Guiding Principles
- A targeted "customer intimacy" approach can work for a small farmer who wants to escape from the mass production/price competition form of farming.

- Selling to restaurants requires
    - Excellent people skills,
    - The ability to provide consistent, exceptional-quality products, and
    - A sufficient understanding of the individual restaurant businesses to accurately predict the products and quantities each will need over the course of the season.

- Developing a successful small farm often requires the careful melding of diverse enterprises into a coherent and profitable system.

Contact Information

Aaron and Kelly Silverman
Creative Growers
Noti, OR

cgrowers@epud.net

Larry Lev
Department of Agricultural and Resource Economics
Ballard Hall, Room 213
Oregon State University
Corvallis, OR 97331-3601

541.737.1417
larry.lev@oregonstate.edu

Farming on the Urban Edge

Ramiro Lobo and Etaferahu Takele

Seabreeze Organic Farm and its Community Supported Agriculture (CSA) program began 14 years ago as a political and environmental statement for owner Stephenie Caughlin. Her effort was meant to create a farm enterprise that would be beneficial to the environment. The farm has evolved into a successful agricultural business that both provides desirable food products and serves as an educational model. Even though the farm is small by most U.S. standards, it is an operation with annual gross revenues exceeding $250,000—a ceiling that defines small-scale operations as established by the USDA's National Commission on Small Farms.

The main enterprises at Seabreeze are a year-round organic vegetable farm and a food delivery system similar to the CSA programs found in the Northeast. The growing part of the business includes production of mixed vegetables, salad greens, herbs, cut flowers, fruits, and some value-added products. The food delivery component of the business includes a variety of products not grown on the farm but which complement the baskets of produce delivered to subscribing customers. These include citrus and a variety of other fruits and value-added products.

Community Supported Agriculture (CSA)—What is It?

CSA is a term used to describe a partnership between farmers and consumers. Under a CSA arrangement, consumers buy agricultural products directly from the farmer, paying for the products in advance at the beginning of the season. Under these circumstances, consumers not only support the farmers' growing operation, but also share in the risks associated with the production of the crops. The farmer, in turn, makes a commitment to produce a diverse and sufficient quantity of high-quality food to satisfy the demands and expectations of consumers.

CSA programs may take many forms and can be initiated either by consumers (the community) or by farmers. Shareholding or participatory CSA programs are usually initiated by a group of consumers who organize to find a suitable piece of land and hire a farmer who will grow the desired mix and quality of produce to satisfy their needs. They then pre-pay all the production expenses and the farmer's salary in equal shares, either as a full payment at the beginning of the season or in installments throughout the growing season. All the crops produced are divided into equal shares among the supporting members.

Subscription-based CSA is a distinct CSA format that is initiated by the grower. This is quite common in California and is the model Seabreeze follows for their food delivery business. Under this arrangement, consumers pay for and receive a weekly delivery of agricultural products that is equivalent to the market value of the products received. Even though growers benefit from having a ready market for their products, they still assume most of the risks associated with the production of the crops. This form of CSA is more of a contractual agreement and the level of consumer participation and involvement in the operation of the farm is much less than that

in the shareholding arrangement described above. This offers more flexibility for consumers because they have the option to pay on a weekly, monthly, quarterly, or annual basis, and they may cancel their subscription at any time if they are not satisfied with the products they get. Customer service and diversity are critical to keeping consumers signed up and Seabreeze has certainly excelled in the quality of their service and the variety they offer.

Risk Factors and Risk Management at Seabreeze Organic Farm

Risk management is an important part of planning at Seabreeze, for whom it means reducing the odds of a financially catastrophic year while allowing for growth. Stephenie considers it an integral part of their overall management plan and a key to the success of the farm. "It's definitely part of it. I wouldn't have survived that long if I hadn't done risk management." Crop and enterprise diversification, market research, market diversification and segmentation, value-added products and activities, and excellent customer service are a few strategies Seabreeze uses. The CSA program or food delivery enterprise has been very useful as a risk management tool because it helps eliminate some of the risks associated with fluctuating market prices. In addition, the diversity of products grown and sold by the farm and the variety of value-added and customer service activities help reduce the risks related to the production and marketing of a specific crop or agricultural product.

Threats to the Business

Rising production costs, predominantly the price of water, is the number one threat to Seabreeze. San Diego County farmers pay an average of $650 per acre foot for irrigation water, making San Diego the county with the highest price for agricultural water in California and perhaps the highest price in the world.

> **"Customers let her know about the 'positives and negatives' of the farm on an ongoing basis."**

The establishment of the new federal organic standards and the fees associated with mandatory certification and state registration constitute the second most important threat to Seabreeze. "My specific business is being organic. A major threat will be affordability of the independent certification per the 1990 Food Act," says Caughlin, referring to the USDA National Organic Program and the California Organic Food Act of 1990. This act sets the guidelines for organic production and use of the label "organic" in the United States and in California. However, organic growers in California are required to register with the state Department of Agriculture in order to produce and market organic products, in addition to the third party certification requirements of the National Organic Program.

The result is that California organic growers that exceed $5,000 in gross sales must pay twice in order to market their product as organic. In response to this, Stephenie foresees major changes to the way Seabreeze does business. "I will probably change my name from organic to sustainable or something else," she says, and she is not alone in this front. "I suspect that we are going to see a big drop in registered organic farms." The implementation of the new organic law as specified in the National Organic Program could greatly affect organic agriculture in San Diego County with its more than 400 registered organic growers. These growers account for nearly 20 percent of all organic producers in California, but the majority of them fall within the $5,000 to $20,000 range in gross sales, making it difficult for them to justify paying for certification fees to meet organic standards.

A third challenge for Seabreeze is the lack of awareness and appreciation among consumers for locally produced food. Of particular importance is "keeping the public awareness up as to the dangers of genetically engineered and chemically produced foods," says Stephenie. Promoting local organic agriculture and the consumption of local, organically produced food is critical for the survival of small farms like hers.

Caughlin thinks that government and bureaucratic agencies will continue to demand and take more money and resources away from farmers with more registration and certification programs and corporate filing fees. "I do feel that in the long run, organic will pull through, surviving the lean times," she says, demonstrating her confidence in the resiliency of farmers.

Competitive Advantages

One of Seabreeze's advantages over similar type operations is that they are both local and organic, yet other important factors giving them an edge include the quality service they provide to their customers, their diverse product mix, and the value-added products and activities they offer. Keeping in touch with consumers is critical for the business to respond to changing needs or to seasonal trends, or to keep consumers/subscribers informed and involved with farm activities. All consumers receive an informative weekly newsletter that includes information about farm activities, recipes to complement the week's delivery and a customized order form they can use to order specific items.

Market Research

Market research is vital for Seabreeze's success, and the farm does some form of it almost on a daily basis. "We pull up the computer (Internet and database), publications, books, newspapers, etc.," Caughlin says about preferred methods for researching market opportunities. Seabreeze keeps an extensive database of consumers and interested individuals, relying heavily on communication and feedback from consumers to help shape their products or services. According to Stephenie, her customers let her know about the "positives and negatives" of the farm on an ongoing basis. Clearly, this is what drives Seabreeze's focus and emphasis on quality and customer service.

Pricing Strategy

Seabreeze relies predominantly on current wholesale organic prices as a baseline for pricing the products they grow. Caughlin does not factor in costs of production in her pricing strategy because she has determined that those costs are very close to what organic wholesale prices are.

This pricing strategy has worked very well for the farm. "My cost would be what the organic wholesale prices are because we're smaller. We're not a large farm. So we're not as efficient," says Stephenie. Seabreeze then adds a premium or markup over the wholesale prices. This pricing strategy is also used to determine the prices for products not grown by the farm. The wholesale price is used as a baseline and then a markup is added on to that baseline price.

Target Market

The target market for the business is usually the local residents of the coastal communities of San Diego County. Stephenie describes these target consumers as being "more affluent, better educated, well-traveled, more environmentally and ecologically aware, more concerned about health and nutrition, and more willing to try new or unusual products." As a result, the core market for the farm operation are the 300-plus consumers listed on the CSA or food delivery program database, with the majority of all subscribers to the program located within 10 miles from the farm. The number of subscribers that actually receive a weekly delivery of produce fluctuates from season to season, but there generally are around 200 weekly deliveries on a year-round basis.

> **There is a direct link, an absolute direct link between this operation, the consumers, and the community.**

Marketing Methods and Market Outlets

The marketing methods used by Seabreeze have changed over the 14-year history of the farm. In the beginning, Seabreeze relied heavily on certified farmers' markets as a main outlet for their products, but gradually decreased the volume sold through them. Selling at farmers' markets was not a profitable option according to Stephenie, citing rising costs of production, transportation costs, marketing expenses, and the proliferation of farmers' markets as the main reasons for the decline of their relative profitability for her business. As a result, Seabreeze has focused more on the CSA program by expanding the number of products offered to include value-added products and by emphasizing quality and customer service.

Seabreeze has expanded their marketing methods to include Internet marketing and mail orders for their value-added products. Both mass email announcements and the farm's website are used to promote the products, events, or activities the farm has to offer. Caughlin says these media have helped create more awareness about the farm but have only generated a limited number of sales. Most product orders from these methods have been from local people with only a few coming from out of state. Despite the slow start, Stephenie sees Internet and email marketing as a strategy worth pursuing mainly because of its cost effectiveness.

Advertising and Promotion

"The marketing that we've done that's been the most successful in the past has been paying a marketing company to actually physically do a doorknob hanger advertising that goes to selected designated neighborhoods in the city," states Stephenie. She is also aware of the cost for this type of advertising: "It's gotten to the point where the farm can no longer afford it because it isn't generating the income." However, she does recognize the importance of advertising and promoting the business. "It's a Catch-22," she says. "We're not generating the income to do the advertising, and without the advertising, you don't get the new people."

But Caughlin recognizes that the relative success of advertising and promotion follows a cyclical pattern, so Seabreeze tries to concentrate advertising and promotion on the seasons that provide a high return for their advertising dollars, usually the spring. Seabreeze has responded to the rising cost of advertising by using other media: their weekly newsletter included with deliveries to subscribers, the Internet, email, and free printed media such as newspapers and magazines. In addition, Stephenie also welcomes any opportunity she gets to obtain free advertising in the form of news stories or reports. She says that she is almost always available for reporters and food editors and relishes her role as the "media farmer" in San Diego.

Measuring Success

Measuring success is one of the most difficult tasks because it is a personal issue that differs from person to person and must be evaluated in terms of the goals and objectives of the operator. Stephenie thinks the best measure of success is that Seabreeze is still in business. After all these years the farm has not lost its focus on making a political statement while providing a source of good quality food, grown in an environmentally sensitive manner. Caughlin is very proud about what the farm has given to the community and the fact that the community recognizes what the farm provides. "I think that we're known in the community at large," she says. "I think they're glad we're here."

Stephenie is very much aware of the need for the business to be sustainable on a financial level. She recognizes that community support through the purchase of Seabreeze's products is critical for financial success. "There is a direct link, an absolute direct link between this operation, the consumers, and the community." Financial success or financial sustainability has been more difficult to achieve, however, and there have been some bad years where she has personally had to finance shortcomings. But, Caughlin reiterates, "We're still here."

Future Plans for the Business/Pending Changes

Clearly, Seabreeze Organic Farm has successfully adapted and responded to changing conditions and trends. However, there are many challenges to overcome and the business must reinvent itself to remain viable. As Stephenie Caughlin says, "It is an ongoing battle…it is always costs, costs, costs! We have to continually find ways to complement the income from the growing side of the business." As a result, there are two strategies and changes that Stephenie feels will enhance the viability of her business:

- Increase Seabreeze's presence on the web and make more efficient use of the Internet: Stephenie feels that expanding their capacity to use the Internet and email more efficiently will yield good returns on their marketing dollars and provide excellent potential for promoting the business and for expanding marketing opportunities.

- Exploit opportunities related to agricultural tourism: Seabreeze is already a popular destination for tours and educational activities, attracting large numbers of visitors from the local area and from outside. Seabreeze must learn to capitalize on this popularity and make money from it.

Guiding Principles

An examination of Seabreeze Organic Farm shows a variety of factors and skills that may determine the relative success of a farm operation.

- Make plans—Have a plan and be prepared for what lies ahead. This provides the flexibility to adjust and to respond to needs, trends, and opportunities that may come down the road.

- Do market research—Maximize the impact of your marketing plan. Research can allow you to identify new opportunities for products or for expansion into new markets.

- Listen to customers—Listen to feedback received from customers. It can provide excellent information for your marketing plan and help keep a check on your business.

- Stay focused—Focus on the goal and objectives you have identified and on the strategies you have chosen to accomplish these goals.

- Have determination—Success is not an overnight occurrence; therefore, you must have the determination to stay on course and implement your strategy despite the many challenges you will encounter.

- Give customer service—Maintain a stable, satisfied customer base. Your current customers can effectively attract new customers from referrals and word-of-mouth advertising.

- Consider product diversification—Diversification can reduce the price and market risks associated with specific products and help introduce value-added products.

- Provide quality—Given the competitive nature of the business, it is critical to provide customers with a quality product and a quality shopping experience.

- Speak up for the industry—It is vital to educate consumers and raise awareness about issues affecting local agriculture. In addition, being available and willing to tell a story is a cost-effective way to promote your business and products.

Contact Information

Stephenie Caughlin
Seabreeze Organic Farm
3909 Arroyo Sorrento Road
San Diego, CA 92130
858.481.0209
seabreezeorganic@sbcglobal.net
www.seabreezed.com

Ramiro Lobo
Cooperative Extension San Diego County
5555 Overland Ave., Building 4
San Diego, CA 92123-1219
858.694.3666
relobo@ucdavis.edu

Etaferahu Takele
Cooperative Extension Riverside County
21150 Box Springs Road
Moreno Valley, CA 92557-8708
909.683.6491, ext. 243
takele@ucrac1.ucr.edu

Nalo Farms

Servicing High-End Restaurants

Stuart T. Nakamoto

Dean Okimoto, the owner-operator of Nalo Farms, has built a highly successful business by supplying excellent-quality salad greens and fresh herbs to many of Hawaii's top restaurants. Dean started with one restaurant in the early nineties and has expanded to where his client list today includes most of Honolulu's top restaurants and chefs, who in turn have won international recognition and numerous culinary awards for innovations such as Pacific Rim cuisine and Hawaii regional cuisine. Many establishments prominently feature Dean's signature product Nalo Greens, a premier salad mix, on their menu.

Nalo Farms has prospered where many other produce growers have been squeezed out of business between high costs of production and low prices for competing products imported from the U.S. west coast. While success is greatly enhanced by having the "rich and famous" as your ultimate clientele, it also takes diligence and hard work to gain and then keep that niche. Dean believes there are three keys to successful niche marketing in a restaurant and resort hotel environment: (1) top quality, (2) consistency, and (3) customer service. All are equally important.

Top Quality

The first key is unsurpassed quality of the product. Dean's products are fresher, and hence tastier and higher yielding than the competition's. Nalo Farms' mission statement reads "We cut in the morning, we pack midday, we deliver in the afternoon, and it's on the customer's plate that night." This emphasis on freshness has meant that even air freight deliveries to a neighbor island have been ruled out. From the Farms' base at Waimanalo (hence the name "Nalo") in rural Oahu, it is at most a one- to two-hour drive to clients in urban Honolulu including Waikiki. Although the inter-island flight itself might be only 30–45 minutes, the logistics of serving markets on other islands could easily add an extra three to four hours to delivery, a margin that Dean felt would be cutting it too close.

Instead, Nalo Farms has formed partnerships with growers on other islands who are willing to grow product according to Nalo Farms' standards and under the Nalo Farms name. On Maui, business arrangements started in 1998 have resulted in a current client list of nearly 20 hotels and restaurants.

Consistency

According to Dean, product consistency and delivery reliability—delivering product in quantities desired and at times promised—are keys for maintaining customers. Clients stay with Nalo Farms because the business is able to consistently give the restaurants what they need, when they need it. However, Dean considers consistency to be one of the high-stress points of his business. He observes that whenever quality is poor, or whenever chefs do not get the supplies they expect, it reflects badly on the business. The reputation of Nalo Farms would be tarnished and the door opened for competitors. Dean compensates by always overproducing, which not only assures supply but also enables only the best product to be marketed.

> **"There are three keys to successful niche marketing in a restaurant and resort hotel environment: top quality, consistency, and customer service."**

Although costly, the strategy has paid off in a sterling reputation for quality and consistency. Despite year-round production in the eight to nine years that Nalo Farms has been in operation, there have been only two instances totaling two weeks in which it could not supply product (both cases because of big storms). Dean recalls "One storm was at election time; we had nine inches of rain. Our fields were all under water. The restaurants understood, but that was major stress, to have to call these guys and tell them we were out of production. What we ended up doing was flying in greens from the West Coast."

Service

The third key is customer service. Here Dean goes beyond day-to-day service to include a longer-term view. Especially when a firm is starting out, if that business is going to build its name and reputation, it is important to be overindulgent as far as customer service goes.

Dean shared an experience from early in the history of Nalo Farms, when he had only three or four accounts. A young chef had just started working in a small Waikiki hotel, after returning to Hawaii from the Pacific Northwest. He contacted Dean and invited him to lunch. Dean enjoyed the meal and thought the chef had promise.

"You know, we are pretty small," the chef started. Then he asked if the restaurant's size would be a problem.

"No," Dean replied, then continued: "I almost lived to regret that because we were making the trip from Waimanalo to Waikiki, 20 miles one way, to deliver a $17 or $20 order."

"But I thought to myself, when you do these restaurants, a lot of times if these guys are good—and I liked this fellow's cooking—then they'll move on to other places. Within a few years, that one restaurant ended up being four accounts totaling $30,000 per month in sales, as that young chef and his workers moved on to larger restaurants. So, you shouldn't overlook a restaurant only because it is small. And, when you go into a restaurant, if there are 'kids' that are interested in what you are doing, take the time to explain it. You never know who is going to go on to be an executive chef at other restaurants, or move up at that restaurant. Never alienate anyone."

Marketing Issues

The right contact. Marketing for Dean starts by using the right contact in the client firm. Dean tries to deal only with the chefs or the person in charge. Especially in corporate-type organizations, there is a tendency for salespeople to be sent to the purchasing managers. "Purchasing managers are not concerned with quality, they are concerned with price. Our Nalo Greens may cost twice as much per pound as a similar imported product, but when you plate it up, it will come out to exactly the same price. You're able to plate up more because it's fresher so has more 'fluff.' You don't have to use as much. One ounce will fill a seven-inch plate and will look really full. The mainland product is flatter and will take about two ounces to fill the plate. So the cost per plate for the chef is essentially the same. Then when they taste it, it sells itself."

In fact, Nalo Farms is at the point where its reputation and its customers do much of the sales work. "We just got a new account when I ran into Al (the restaurant owner) and we started talking. Al told me about recently eating Nalo Greens at another restaurant. He said, 'The flavor is so much more intense than what we're serving at our restaurant. We're buying (U.S.) mainland greens. Then I found out that you get more yield from the Nalo Greens. Why don't we take a look at it?' So we talked some more and I got the business."

Market research. Dean and his staff are constantly talking to the chefs to find what their needs are and what they want. It's also important to be computer literate or have staff that can use computers. One big use is to track trends and busy seasons. For example, on Oahu the peak season is from November to mid-January whereas on Maui, the busy period is between January and March. This may be due to a different visitor-to-resident mix of diners. Consequently, the company gears up planting at different times for the different islands. Maui clients also seem to be more price sensitive, perhaps due to the much larger size of the Oahu market.

> "...always overproducing ... not only assures supply, but also enables only the best product to be marketed."

Dean considers the San Francisco area to be a mecca of new agricultural products. He often travels there to find new ideas. "There are some open markets that are just humongous," he says. "There are probably 150 different varieties of just tomatoes. It's fantastic, it's unbelievable."

Charity events. It is also part of Nalo Farms' business philosophy to give back to the community. "You've got to give back to get back," says Dean. "Besides, when we do these charity events, we generally gain business from that. At the beginning, we probably gained one or two customers at every event. It's not only the people who patronize the event, but also the people who are serving. So, we not only give back, but it can make good business sense as well."

Business expansion. Dean does not consider any farmer in Hawaii as his competition. "Hawaii imports so much—I consider imported mainland produce as my competition. That is what I work towards, buying less from the mainland and having people buy more locally." Toward that end, Nalo Farms is considering expanding its operations beyond its restaurant and resort hotel niche, perhaps into mainstream supermarkets. Dean admits it is an attractive idea, but the main problem is he does not want to have the same product for the general public as is in the restaurants. As Dean puts it, "We would shoot ourselves in the foot if we did that. Part of the reason the restaurants are using Nalo Greens is because it is not widely available in the market. We may offer a different mix and call it something like 'Nalo Wonder Greens' so people are aware of the difference."

Key Points/Guiding Principles

- High-end niche markets, in this case top restaurants and resort hotels, are attractive, potentially lucrative opportunities. Top quality, consistency in quality and supply, and customer service are keys to establishing and maintaining a market presence.

- The firm's good name and high reputation are powerful assets that must be protected.

- Price is not necessarily the most important factor to buyers. Instead, a focus on value—the perceived benefits for the price paid—can be more important.

- Planned overproduction can be a useful risk management tool; it assures adequate supplies and enhances high quality as well.

Contact Information

Dean Okimoto
Nalo Farms, Inc.
41-574 Makakalo St.
Waimanalo, HI 96795

808.259.7698
nalofarms@aol.com

Stuart T. Nakamoto
Department of Human Nutrition, Food, and
 Animal Sciences (UH-HNFAS)
University of Hawaii
1955 East-West Road, AgSci 314B
Honolulu, HI 96822

808.956.8125
snakamo@hawaii.edu

Kona Coffee for the Japanese Market

Kent Fleming and Stuart T. Nakamoto

The agriculture in Kona, a mountainous region on the western side of the Island of Hawaii (i.e., the Big Island), is known primarily for its coffee production. Until recently, Kona was the only location in the United States where coffee was grown commercially. Kona Coffee is an internationally renowned gourmet coffee. Production, harvesting, and processing are all done by hand on small farms averaging about four acres in size, and the coffee quality is carefully monitored and controlled. The name "Kona Coffee" is a federal trademark, and certification is strictly enforced by the state. For these reasons, the supply of Kona Coffee is low relative to world demand, and this coffee can be sold at a premium. Kona Coffee and Jamaican Blue Mountain are currently the most expensive coffees in the world, selling for as much as $50 per pound in some specialty coffee retail stores.

While the final product receives a high price, the labor-intensive nature of its production means that costs are also relatively high. Farmers rely on transient, skilled, hand-harvest labor that is often difficult to obtain, especially during the peak of the harvest season. Indeed, costs are so high that the average "farm gate" price that growers receive is often less than the economic cost of production, which is about $1.10 per pound of cherry. Further, in spite of the relatively high demand for their product, farm gate prices can be extremely volatile, ranging from below the $0.40 per pound harvest cost to $1.75 per pound of cherry.

Few if any producers are economically viable in the long run unless they take their product beyond the cherry stage. The next stage is the parchment or washed and dried stage. While this product will provide improved returns, there are several other stages culminating in a roasted and ground product that often offers better profit opportunities.

Innovative Niche Marketing: The Love Farm Approach

The Love Farm is a typical, small coffee farm in Kona. What distinguishes Ken Love's from others, even from those that do carry the processing beyond merely harvesting and delivering cherry

to a processor, is his focus on innovative niche marketing. The capital investment necessary for the washing, drying, milling, and roasting equipment to take cherry to the roasted coffee bean is exorbitant and well beyond the resources of the typical, relatively small Kona producer. Love is able to avoid this capital expense by being an active member of a farmers' marketing cooperative that processes members' coffee cherry and then either sells the roasted coffee for them or returns their coffee to them to market on their own.

Ken Love designs all of his own labels on his desktop computer and prints them using an inexpensive color printer and very high quality label paper from Japan. He packages his own roasted coffee (as beans or ground coffee) in small (from two ounces to two pounds), air-tight colorful foil packages. Coffee is then sold in one of two ways: (1) in the manner of a traditional estate-branded coffee in local retail outlets, in high-end restaurants and hotels, and on the Internet, or (2) as a custom product designed for a specific customer. In the latter case, the label focuses on the buyer rather than in describing the coffee roast or variety or the farm. People wishing to give presents (e.g., an unusual favor for a wedding party or a distinctive gift for business clients or a unique Hawaiian souvenir for friends) can have their name and any special event information printed on a label designed for the giver's purposes. Specific labels are then affixed to the size of packages desired by the gift giver.

Ken Love has an ongoing personal fascination with Japan and Japanese culture. He speaks some Japanese and has had business interests there for many years. He visits Japan frequently and keeps current on Japanese social, economic, and cultural trends. His orientation allows him to appreciate the Japanese emphasis on gift giving, with the attendant demand for high quality and the importance of presentation through packaging. His insight into this aspect of the Japanese psyche enabled him to perceive the opportunity to provide the kind of gift Japanese customers would desire.

Hawaii, and Kona in particular, annually receives many thousands of visitors from Japan and they constitute an important potential market that Ken has managed to tap successfully. Because of his understanding of the Japanese, he empathizes with their situation as visitors in Kona. Japan Airlines (JAL) flies thousands of Japanese tourists directly from Tokyo to Kona. The arriving passengers are whisked off to nearby Japanese-owned resorts, where guests remain isolated from everyday life in Kona for the duration of their stay, enjoying the weather, the beach, and golf. They are then returned to the airport where they can catch their JAL direct flight back to Japan. This tourism approach leads to (1) local resentment that all the revenues flow in a closed loop back to Japan and (2) dissatisfaction by the visitors who, while acknowledging that Kona is a "nice place," complain that there is "nothing to do" in Kona.

> **Love's most interesting agri-tourism enterprise is his coffee tree rental program.**

Again, Love recognizes a marketing opportunity. He takes Japanese visitors up into the hills about 25 miles south of the airport to visit his farm. His familiarity with the Japanese language and customs puts the visitors at ease and allows them to be more open to the agricultural scene and other rural amenities. His website and printed materials are in both English and Japanese.

Love's most interesting agri-tourism enterprise is his coffee tree rental program. A person can rent a tree for $1,100 per year. In return, the renter receives 50 seven-ounce bags (22 pounds total) of roasted "coffee from the rented tree." Since an average tree produces only the equivalent of about two to three pounds of roasted coffee, the amount provided to a tree renting customer comes from the rented tree plus nine or ten of the farm's other trees. Each bag comes with a label of the customer's choice. This amounts to a coffee price of $50 per pound, equal to the highest U.S. mainland retail price and twice as much as the best Kona retail price. In addition, each customer is provided a location on the farm's website where s/he can go to see a picture of the rented tree. A renter can visit his or her tree at any time, and depending upon the time of year, can prune, harvest, or otherwise care for the tree.

Finally, Love Farm's longer-term goals include diversifying the operation by moving into exotic tropical fruits. Ken has identified over 100 fruits and nuts growing in the Kona area alone, ranging from more familiar products such as pineapples, macadamias, oranges, and papayas to mangos, guava, and lychee to wampi, rambutan, jaboticaba, and kitembilla. Ken is experimenting with several outlets and ways to add value to the fruit by use of point-of-purchase materials, packaging, and processing—he has over 70 different products. He has also created a poster *Exotic Fruit from the Big Island of Hawaii* and features many fruits on his website at www.mycoffee.net/fruitindex.html.

Threats to Business

Growers are vulnerable to the usual vagaries of the weather, pests, and other natural phenomena, as well as being vulnerable to the decreasing availability and the increasingly higher cost of water, land, and labor. An inadequate supply of skilled harvest labor will be an increasing problem, especially as more coffee comes into production in the Kona "coffee belt" region. Major production risks for the industry are the twig hole borer and the virulent Kona Coffee Root-knot Nematode, for which there is no remedy except to replant the infested acreage with expensive grafted rootstock.

> **"Each customer is provided a location on the farm's website where s/he can go to see a picture of the rented tree."**

In the longer run, weakening Hawaiian and Japanese economies are a serious threat. Hawaii's economy is important because the state must continue to enforce Kona Coffee certification. As the economy weakens, there will be calls for expenditure cutbacks. Without the reputation of the Kona name, Love Farm's coffee could not attract high prices, and therefore it is critical to be able to have the state inspectors to assure buyers that Kona Coffee is, indeed, produced in Kona.

The strength of the Japanese economy is critical because a large part of Love Farm's marketing is based on having a healthy Japanese visitor industry. With less disposable income, potential visitors may be lured to other destinations closer to Japan or they may continue to visit Hawaii, but be less inclined to purchase Kona Coffee-related gifts, including renting trees. Related to this, a serious threat is not being able to generate an adequate cash flow for proper advertising and public relations in Japan.

Risk Management Tools

In the short run, Love Farm's biggest risk involves coffee pest management. Love needs to stay abreast of current findings and regulations. To help manage this risk, the farm always has additional coffee nursery stock ready for planting in the orchard should something happen to the producing trees. However, Ken does not view nematodes as being as serious a threat to his operation as it is to others, given his method of operation.

The farm is managing longer-term risks by diversifying from coffee into other tropical fruits. Ken is always looking at unusual ways to market fruits and add value to them as he does with coffee. With his knowledge of markets and his costs, Ken sees a given acreage as being potentially more profitable if planted in the appropriate fruit trees rather than in coffee.

Competitive Edge

Love Farm's competitive edge comes from knowing Japanese customers better than anyone else in Kona and from being able to conceive and implement creative marketing ideas for the coffee they produce. Like many farmers in Kona, the farm offers a quality coffee certified to have been grown in Kona. But what it offers beyond this product are options and choices for how customers receive this coffee. Ken's customized labels are available if clients order ahead of time, or they can choose from a standard list. "We allow the customer to feel very much involved in the farm, to take some ownership in our efforts, even to the extent of allowing them to 'rent' a tree and maintain it as much as they may like," said Ken. Admittedly, this involvement is mostly symbolic, but customers genuinely feel that this farm is "their coffee farm." In some elemental way it is one of their psychological homes away from their real home.

Market Research

Ken Love's overall marketing plan emerged from his knowledge and understanding of the Japanese customer. By trying to see the world the way the customer does, ongoing research consists of spending time talking to customers and asking questions about their experience with Love's coffee and with other competitors'. This information helps Ken to refine the operation. The Love Farm also gives samples away in stores to help create a dialogue.

Business Sustainability

Ken believes that the business model underlying the Love Farm is sustainable, "But *only* if we are continually looking at new niches in which to market. We constantly strive for even more unusual and creative marketing approaches. The competition is fierce, and there are many large concerns that sell well under their actual cost of production in order to gain market share. We have chosen to concentrate our efforts in Japan and Europe with unusual marketing, rather than to try to compete locally. Each product has many attributes, including price. We do not compete on price."

When asked how he measures success, Ken indicated that it is hard to do so only by the bottom line—whether the coffee enterprise is covering all its expenses—since almost everything goes back into building the business. The farm has a positive cash flow, but Ken is not sure at this time whether their operation is actually economically profitable, covering all invested capital and labor. "A better measure of success at this point in the life of the business may be the positive feedback we receive from customers. For now, that is the most rewarding aspect of the business—and the feeling that we are making progress in the right direction." The Loves also believe that they are helping their rural community be more sustainable by providing tourists with a reason to visit their farm—such as tending their rented trees.

Product Pricing

Pricing is governed more by market factors than by the cost of coffee production in Kona. Coffee prices there are supported by certification as Kona Coffee, whose limited production region and supply generally provide protection from downward price movements. Most growers would prefer to compete on factors other than price, although there are many who promote their coffee simply as being the lowest-priced certified Kona Coffee.

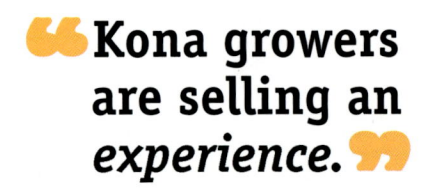

> **Kona growers are selling an *experience.***

However, quite unlike Kona Coffee, fruit are perishable and relatively price sensitive. Therefore, Ken's fruit prices are set more according to what the market will accept. "We try to keep the prices for more unusual fruit relatively lower than for the more common fruits, so that people will try the unfamiliar. On more common fruits such as avocado, we work with merchants to promote sales." They will also drop prices every so often so that vendors will feature the fruit in advertised sales.

Future Business Changes

At present, coffee for the Japanese market is their core business. The Loves have been planting coffee trees as if their business will continue to grow and provide quality coffee products that are unusual in their packaging. "We may try to change our coffee packaging for the local market to make it more unusual and thus more competitive locally. We would like to try a package that would have some kind of other use after the coffee is gone." Overall, growth is planned to drive their core business and this is mainly limited by funds available for additional promotion.

In the long run, perhaps the greatest potential for real growth will be in the marketing of locally produced tropical fruits, especially relatively rare fruits. The Love Farm plans to build on what they have learned with coffee marketing by broadening their focus to include the local and U.S. mainland visitor markets. "Kona Coffee will then be just one item in the basket of our offerings. With processed products, we plan on starting an additional website and developing collateral for our rare fruit. Preliminary explorations have been very positive. There are many stores now asking for our fruit products, and we cannot produce them fast enough to fulfill the orders we have created simply by investigating the potential markets. We need to continue to develop the infant market for rare tropical fruits."

To accomplish this, the Love Farm probably needs outside start-up funds, perhaps through a market development grant of some sort. Along this line, they will continue to work closely with the University of Hawaii's researchers and extension specialists and agents at the Kona Experiment Station where Ken is currently engaged in a tropical fruit marketing development project. Ken is the vice president and past treasurer of the Kona Pacific Farmers Cooperative and president of the Tropical Fruit Growers Association, keeping him actively involved and aware of future developments in the business.

Guiding Principles Gleaned

In summary, there are at least four main components of the Love's Farm strategy that stand out.

- Love's whole farm strategy is essentially a *marketing strategy*. Production issues must, of course, be monitored, but there is not an overriding concern either to maximize (or even optimize) yield or to minimize costs. The farm product (coffee cherry) will be processed to the final roasted coffee stage, then packaged on farm to capture more of the added value. All the coffee grown and processed will be sold at retail values. The focus is on marketing the Kona Coffee, not on growing it.

- Competition is with other Kona Coffees, but it is *not price competition*. Love competes on some of the other product attributes, such as how the coffee is presented to the consumer, whether it be in a package selected by the consumer or from his own rented tree. The coffee produced is a quality product with the Kona appellation, but there are hundreds of other farmers producing a very similar product. Perhaps a "cupper" or professional taster might subjectively differentiate among the various Kona estate coffees from one year or another. But for all practical purposes, only a few of these hundreds of estate coffees have significantly branded or otherwise differentiated their product by, for example, the coffee's particular point of origin or its product qualities.

- The Kona name is critical for all Kona Coffee growers. Without it, their coffee would be worth half as much or less. It can be argued that the Kona location produces better coffee, but it is also a fact that visitors who enjoy the experience of visiting Kona are an important component of the buyers of Kona Coffee. Essentially, Kona growers are selling an *experience*, and to the extent that they can further enhance the experience, such as through a farm visit, the greater will be their competitive advantage.

- Competition is further defined by the particular market target: Japan. Kona Coffee, packaged appropriately, is marketed to Japanese consumers that have visited Kona, Hawaii. Love, given his personal interests, has developed an exceptional understanding of and appreciation for the Japanese consumer. *Understanding the Japanese customer's "needs"* gives him a competitive advantage, relative to the other Kona farmers who could provide a similar product. In short, he is freed from competing in the local market for local buyers or for visitors from the U.S. mainland. These markets are nearly saturated and usually involve competing largely on price.

Contact Information

Ken Love
Love Family Farms
PO Box 1242
Captain Cook, HI 96704

808.323.2417
Ken@mycoffee.net
www.mycoffee.net

Kent Fleming
Department of Tropical Plant and Soil
   Sciences (UH-TPSS)
University of Hawaii
Kona Extension Office
PO Box 208
Kealakekua, HI 96750
808.322.9136
fleming@hawaii.edu

Stuart T. Nakamoto
Department of Human Nutrition, Food, and
   Animal Sciences (UH-HNFAS)
University of Hawaii
1955 East-West Road, AgSci 314B
Honolulu, HI 96822
808.956.8125
snakamo@hawaii.edu

Cattail Creek Farm

Building a Successful Part-Time Farm through Informal Collaborative Agreements

Larry Lev

John Neumeister was raised on a part-time sheep farm in Ohio and has been producing lambs for much of his adult life. When he bought his small farm in western Oregon in 1983, he planned on producing blueberries. But he never quite had the funds to get started. Instead, he stayed with what he knew—sheep. He farms part time and has a full-time day job. Lamb production is a common enterprise in Oregon with more than 2,800 farms selling sheep according to the 1997 Census of Agriculture. John's farm is set apart from these other farms through his marketing channels and the collaborative arrangements that he has forged over the years.

The United States Department of Agriculture classifies John's farm among the 63 percent of all farms that are "rural residences" rather than "commercial" or "intermediate" farms. On average, these rural residence farms lose money. Their owners are more interested in lifestyle and quality of life than they are in income. Although John clearly values the lifestyle he has developed, he is also proud that his farm turns a profit.

Lamb Production

The actual farming operation is small. John maintains a herd of 35 ewes on his 17-acre farm near Eugene. In 2001, he sold 40 lambs from this farm. Self-imposed limitations or constraints he has placed on the production side of the operation are the following: (1) no borrowed money, (2) no hired labor, and (3) no grazing of animals except on his own pastures. It is quite common in western Oregon for sheep to graze on harvested grass seed fields—something that John rejects because of concerns for the chemicals used in grass seed production). As a result, John will not expand lamb production beyond its current level.

Here is how John characterizes his production approach:

"Our goal is to produce healthy food in a way that is sustainable for our soil and water resources. We care for our lambs within the livestock raising standards of the Humane Society of America. We feed them a vegetarian diet of lush pasture, supplemented with kelp, hay, and whole natural or organic grains. We never use GMO feed, hormones, steroids, or antibiotics, nor have pesticides ever been applied to our farms."

The Larger Lamb Marketing Enterprise

Through a recently developed collaborative arrangement with another farm, John brokers many more lambs under his farm's name than he produces. Under this venture, the Cattail Creek Farm brand expanded to sell 300 lambs in 2001 (and even more in 2002). The other 260 lambs (or 87% of the total) are all produced by what John refers to as "our sister farm, Rain Sheep Ranch." This arrangement is a simple handshake deal with Rain Sheep producing the lambs and John brokering them.

Why does the much smaller partner provide the marketing identity for this collaborative agreement? There are two primary reasons. First, John's partner is primarily interested in development of prime breeding stock and specialty wool, with meat sales being a supplementary business. Second, John has a much greater fascination and interest with the meat side of the industry than does his partner. So John finds customers for all of the lambs, earns a respectable brokerage fee for himself, and provides Rain Sheep with a stable price that is always significantly above the volatile wholesale market. Rain Sheep provides a high-quality product that maintains the Cattail Creek reputation, and it still has the time to focus on other enterprises.

Pricing and Identity Preservation

All of the lambs sold under the Cattail Creek brand earn top dollar from commercial customers who are looking for high-quality products. The identity-preserved Cattail Creek meat earns John more than double what he would earn on the wholesale market when it's down and slightly more when it's up. He also sells at a set price and doesn't have to concern himself with the substantial price fluctuations in the wholesale market.

In pricing his meat, John does not pay any attention to the commercial lamb market, which he feels delivers a very different product. Cattail Creek Lamb is dry aged for six days, cut, wrapped, and delivered the next day. Commercial lamb in the Northwest is not dry aged and the majority of it is processed out of state (or country) and shipped in. John fixes his price on his perception of what the market will bear. At one stage he had almost as many prices as he did customers. He has since moved to a standard price for all. He does still differentiate, however, by giving his better customers superior service and higher quality.

Marketing and Customer Service

In going from 40 lambs to 300 lambs, John had to greatly expand his roster of clients. He has one restaurant customer in California (serviced by air freight), but all of his other customers are in Oregon (25 restaurants and 7 retail outlets). John provides a product with guaranteed and consistent quality and on-time delivery. Each customer receives special and individual treatment to make sure that the cuts John provides are what the customer needs to succeed. These cuts can vary substantially from restaurant to restaurant and John is willing to work with each client to get the cuts right. Within a restaurant, John makes a point of developing a relationship with everyone in the restaurant who is actively involved in the operation. Generally this means the top six people. This helps to protect him from competitors.

Many of his customers are clustered in the Portland area. Somewhat surprisingly, he found that far from worrying about exclusivity, his initial customers played a key role in finding him new business. This provides a great example of direct markets operating in an unexpected fashion. John is also constantly on the lookout for customers in more remote locations (such as the Oregon Coast and Ashland in southern Oregon) and innovative ways for getting his fresh products to these clients. While John enjoys the close relationships he develops with commercial customers, he does not actively pursue locker lamb sales to individuals.

Marketing to restaurants and retail stores takes time. Each week John works the phones by calling all of his customers and asking what they need. He then pieces together the orders to represent whole animals if at all possible. One lesson he has learned over time is that the higher-value cuts need to be sold fresh while the lower value cuts can be stored frozen for a period of time. He views this whole process as a kind of a puzzle and enjoys doing it every week although he recognizes this activity might drive others crazy. He now confirms orders with three clients by email, but still finds that he makes at least one call or face-to-face contact on each order just to make sure everything is as it needs to be.

Making the actual deliveries, most of which are 90 miles away, and talking to his customers face-to-face represents a major time commitment he must make. To reduce his time devoted to marketing, John has developed a unique marketing collaboration with a farmer who sells

> **"Informal, voluntary collaborations can make important contributions to a business by providing access to additional resources and expertise."**

pastured poultry to similar upscale clients. Aaron Silverman (see Creative Growers, p. 8) owns a refrigerated truck that the two of them rotate on alternating weeks to deliver product to their overlapping customer base. In making sales calls and deliveries, John promotes Aaron's product and Aaron does the same for John's lamb. The key foundation of this collaboration is that each has complete confidence in both the decision making and the salesmanship of the other. As a result, each has cut in half the number of days spent on deliveries.

Strengths of the Business

To an outside observer, John's ability to collaborate with other producers is an important strength. Reflecting on these two informal, collaborative relationships, he observes, "Much more than with employees, this type of relationship always keeps us on our best behavior. I really like how that feels." John is open to developing other collaborative arrangements in the future because he recognizes how useful they are for someone in his situation. Although he has only a small farming operation, by working with other producers he is able to draw on a bigger pool of resources and expertise.

When directly questioned about the greatest strength of his business, John provides an intriguing answer: "It's probably that I'm not in business to make money. I'm in business to enjoy the rural lifestyle and, as it turns out, to enjoy the entrepreneurial part of making sales." This allows John to stay nimble and react to the needs of his clients. By focusing on continuing to do things the way he wants—he is an admitted perfectionist—he doesn't have to worry about declining standards or the urge to expand the business much beyond its current scale. Thus, the business is a successful and sustainable part-time operation.

Threats to the Business

The greatest threat that John identified would be his slaughterhouse going out of business. John is already driving 70 miles one way to have his animals slaughtered. Skilled meat cutters are increasingly rare in the Pacific Northwest. Since he is not a big enough client to keep a slaughter facility in business, he cannot control whether this facility will remain open. Because of how busy the facility is, John must schedule his animals far in advance and stick pretty close to the number allotted to him.

His second concern is a prolonged economic downturn. Because upscale restaurants are his primary market, the worry is that people will stop eating in these restaurants or that they will move down the menu to lower-priced items—since lamb dishes are frequently among the more expensive entrees. Immediately following 9/11/01, he noticed a dramatic slowdown in his restaurant orders. As one response to this threat, John has begun to pay more attention to developing the retail store component of his clientele. He believes this added diversity in markets will dampen the swings in demand for his product.

Third among his worries would be losing customers to a competitor. John recognizes that someone else could squeeze him out and therefore he has to continually maintain/upgrade the quality of his product and services.

Guiding Principles and Key Lessons

- Successful part-time enterprises can be built to reflect the values, passions, and interests of the owners.

- Informal, voluntary collaborations can make important contributions to a business by providing access to additional resources and expertise.

- Niche markets exist for high-quality products that are supported with superb service.

- Diversifying market outlets reduces overall marketing risks.

Contact Information

John Neumeister
Cattail Creek Farm
95363 Grimes Road
Junction City, OR 97448

541.998.8505
jneumeister@earthlink.net
www.cattailcreekfarm.com

Larry Lev
Department of Agricultural and Resource
   Economics
Ballard Hall, Room 213
Oregon State University
Corvallis, OR 97331-3601

541.737.1417
larry.lev@oregonstate.edu

Marketing "Natural" Beef

Rod Sharp

In the fall of 1995, many cow-calf producers from the Tri River area in western Colorado attended a grazing conference in Delta, Colorado. The featured speakers were Oregonians Doc and Connie Hattfield, who discussed how they and approximately 10 other ranchers from Oregon were marketing their beef directly to restaurants, health food stores, and other retail outlets in the Northwest. They also talked about a contract they had to export beef to Japan.

The Hattfields' presentation stirred interest in developing the same type of markets in Colorado. Over 50 western Colorado ranchers began attending Cooperative Extension-facilitated monthly meetings to explore opportunities to enhance their profitability. Discussions at the initial meetings centered around ways for the group of producers to set an asking price for their beef products instead of taking what the market was offering. They were very frustrated with the commodity market prices of beef and live cattle and wanted to investigate using an integrated approach to direct market their beef. In fact, they wanted to position themselves so they could guarantee a price to the rancher based on $85 per hundredweight live weight for a market-ready steer.

To develop the market, they knew they had to generate and sell a differentiated product. Early on they decided to capitalize on "natural" beef products that are grown without hormones or feed additives. They also hoped to market the fact that the cattle were born and raised on high mountain pastures in western Colorado since many of the ranchers practice Holistic Resource Management (HRM) and wanted to sell the principles of HRM through their products.

These meetings continued for about a year and a half before a group of 23 ranchers officially formed the Rocky Mountain Beef (RMB) Cooperative. Before deciding to be a cooperative, they explored the pros and cons of four different business organizations (partnerships, limited partnerships, corporations, and cooperatives). Based on their business goals, they determined that a cooperative made the most sense. Some of its characteristics that appealed to the group included member ownership and control, return of profits to the members, and voluntary membership.

> **"The biggest threat to the Cooperative is the high cost of processing."**

From there, the ranchers contacted the Rocky Mountain Farmers Union Cooperative Development Center in Denver for financial and technical assistance. With the Center's help, their papers were filed with the secretary of state to form a legally functioning, agricultural marketing cooperative. The Center also assisted the group in developing their first application for membership and their disclosure statement.

To be a part of the Cooperative, a rancher had to pay an initial fee of $250 and be willing to follow some agreed upon policies. Each member had to (1) designate animals for common feedlot every month to guarantee year-round supplies, (2) raise animals according to the "Natural Beef" guidelines, (3) insure animals had 0.3 to 0.35 inches of fat thickness, (4) keep animals on feed at least 90 days, and (5) make certain animals were not more than two years old. To ensure freshness and better control of supplies, members also agreed to sell everything frozen.

About half of the original group dropped out for various reasons. Four ranchers left very early and formed their own cooperative known as Homestead Natural Beef. Homestead had run cattle together before in a common grazing pool and had a long history of cooperation. Several other producers were not willing to keep attending all the meetings. Others were not willing to put in the time, effort, and money the Cooperative needed to get started because until markets were established, very few animals would be affected. These ranchers felt the benefits would not justify their participation in the Cooperative.

Threats to the Business

The biggest threat, both short- and long-term, to the Cooperative is the high cost of processing. Local processors are small and concentrate primarily on small-scale custom processing of domestic animals and wild game. Typically, the cost to have cattle processed in these small plants averages about $250 per head compared with $85 to $90 per head in an Exel or IBP plant. This large difference in processing costs makes it difficult to compete even when premiums are available. Larger plants also have the advantage of selling their by-products (hides, offal, etc.) to established markets to help cover the costs of processing.

Forming alliances with some of the local processors may help mitigate this threat. RMB wants to show the small-scale processor that working together will ensure volume throughout the year to help offset some of the ups and downs in custom and game processing.

Another threat to the success of the Cooperative is their problem with inventory management. RMB producers have always had good demand and contracts for the higher-quality cuts. However, they have had difficulty selling hamburger and other lower-quality products at the price necessary to meet profit goals. Inventory of these cuts builds up over time and they are forced to sell at a discounted price, thus reducing the total value of the animal.

RMB is working to establish contracts with food distributors to sell whole carcasses. Another strategy to help with inventory control is to sell lower-end cuts on the open commodity market and establish a higher price on the other cuts, especially the medium-range cuts.

The inventory problem of lower-valued cuts has also resulted in increasing debt to the members. A member delivers an animal to the Cooperative with expectations of a certain return on that animal. But selling the lower-end cuts at a substantial discount or keeping the cuts in cold storage has substantially affected the returns to the producers. With some of the members, this has taken some of the luster off the project, and it makes it difficult to get members to designate cattle for the feedlot to ensure a consistent year-round supply of product. The Cooperative is bringing in new members from other adjacent counties to increase volume and expand markets. By working cooperatively with other Western Slope ranches, RMB hopes to increase profits and reduce debt to members.

Another concern or possible longer-term threat is the rumor that Exel is attempting to purchase Coleman Meats, the primary "natural" meat company in the region and a direct competitor with RMB. The RMB membership feels it would be difficult to compete with the larger, more efficient processors.

There is a potential trend for each small geographic area to organize its own small group of producers to direct market beef. The possibility of several small groups competing with each other is another possible threat to RMB. Members of the Cooperative and others are encouraging these groups to work together rather than compete for the same markets.

> **"Generating enough seed money to get a cooperative going is critical."**

Product Pricing

Originally, the members wanted to establish a price for the live animal at $85 per hundredweight and then calculate backwards to price the individual cuts. Based on the yield of live to carcass and carcass to products, the price per pound of individual cuts was set. Cooperative members chose $85 per hundredweight because they knew it would cost more to feed cattle naturally and the $85 figure would provide the profit margin to stay in business and generate a fair return on their investment.

They soon realized that the retail outlets they were selling to were uncomfortable paying a fixed price for beef. These outlets expected the price to fluctuate based on the commodity price. So, RMB started pricing their beef based on a $0.12 to $0.15 per pound premium over published commodity market prices.

They even had some problems with the premium pricing. RMB dry ages their beef for 14 days before delivery. It was a struggle determining what the yield was on dry-aged beef because all the yield literature is based on beef that is not aged. The industry yield information is also based on an industry average and RMB producers felt that their cattle performed better than the average. Using their own records, they calculated their actual yield to set the price.

Competitive Edge

Several factors were identified that provide RMB members a competitive edge. The first is that they produce a "natural" product and have an official USDA Certified Natural label. Growing concerns by consumers about health and food safety have increased demand for natural and organic products, so positioning themselves for this expanding market is a real advantage.

RMB is also doing a good job promoting how and where animals are raised. Marketing to local retail outlets has also been an advantage. These buyers like to support local agriculture to preserve open space and the ranching landscape that communities value.

A consistent high-quality product is another advantage of the Cooperative. They have a very good feeding program and being small, they are able to select cattle out of the feedlot in optimum condition for slaughter. Many consumers also prefer the tenderness and flavor of beef that has been dry aged.

Marketing Research

RMB has been involved with both formal and informal marketing research. With the Rocky Mountain Farmers Union and Colorado State University Cooperative Extension, they have conducted formal research on (1) consumer interest and acceptance of natural beef products, (2) willingness to pay a premium for these products, (3) the feasibility of larger-scale processing plants including a multispecies plant, and (4) the feasibility of outsourcing the processing to larger plants outside the local area.

Informally, RMB continually compares its products with its competitors'. They focus primarily on the types of natural beef products being offered and their pricing.

Changes for the Future

RMB is working to develop hamburger markets in the region's ski resorts. They are looking at selling their cull cows through this market. The network and cooperation developed by being members of the Cooperative has also encouraged pool marketing of other animals not sold through RMB (culls, rejects, etc.), shared purchase of inputs (feed, for example), and other opportunities to work together for the benefit of all. In fact, these relationships may eventually have a bigger impact in generating profits for the individual producers than will their cooperative marketing of natural beef.

Some Things Learned

- Always make sure the product being sold is of the highest quality.

- Look for growing markets (natural, lean, dry-aged, locally grown, etc.) based on consumer demand and long-range outlook.

- Be aware that the cost of production and efficiency are still important in generating profits.

- Be flexible enough to make changes in the business as the environment changes.

- A cooperative takes a lot of time and effort by everyone, but this is especially true for key members that provide leadership for the group.

- Generating enough seed money to get a cooperative going is critical. The most common reason for failure is the lack of capital.

- The meat business is not easy. It is highly competitive and retail outlets and other businesses are not always loyal or reliable.

- It is important to involve agencies such as Cooperative Extension that can provide technical assistance along the way.

Contact Information

Tom Wise
10230 Bostwick Park Road
Montrose, CO 81401

Rod Sharp
Colorado State University
Cooperative Extension
2764 Compass Dr., Suite 232
Grand Junction, CO 81506

970.245.9149
rsharp@coop.ext.colostate.edu

The Holualoa Kona Coffee Company

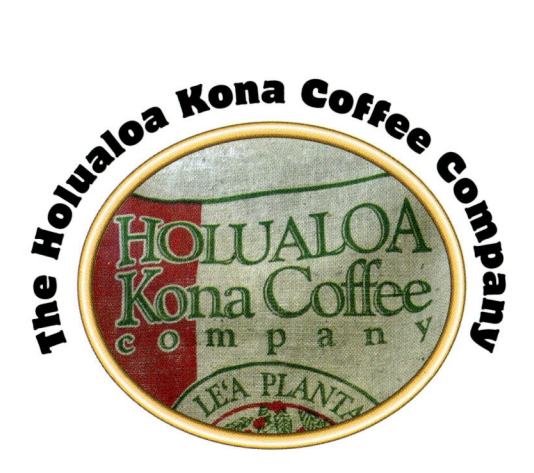

Marketing Memorable Experiences and High-Quality Products

Stuart T. Nakamoto and Kent Fleming

The Kona Le'a Plantation is perched on the slopes of Mount Hualalai, overlooking Kailua Bay on the Island of Hawaii. It is the home of Holualoa Kona Coffee Company, a family business owned by Desmond and Lisen Twigg-Smith. Tourists venture forth from their seaside resorts in Kailua-Kona for a 10-minute journey up a narrow, winding country road into lush, tropical forests and Kona Coffee country to visit this place.

The operation consists of a number of buildings set amidst 16 acres of coffee trees. The property is a narrow, pie-shaped parcel running *mauka* (toward the mountain) of historic Mamalahoa Highway. As explained to farm visitors, this unusual layout stems from the *ahupua'a*, or ancient Hawaiian system of land division, where chiefs would control parcels running from the mountaintop to the sea.

The buildings include a wet mill, parchment drying and storage shed, dry mill, warehouses, roasting room, and packing room/retail outlet. Some antique equipment is displayed in an open garage where a bunch of ripening bananas hangs from the rafters. The owners' former residence is also on the property. It is surrounded by gardens with exotic plants such as taro, pineapple, hibiscus, gardenia, flowering ginger and heliconia, 50-foot tall mango, avocado, and jacaranda trees, cacao, and bananas.

Visitors are often met by one of the Twigg-Smiths or one of the employees. Wesley Summer, who also doubles as a master roaster/resident caretaker, was our guide when a group of us recently visited the operation. The informal tour follows the journey of the coffee bean starting from the tree and ending at the cup. Coffee is an attractive tree growing 10 to 15 feet tall, with glossy, dark green leaves. "In the spring, it looks like it snowed when all the coffee blossoms are blooming," said Wes. The green fruits develop to about the size of a fingernail and usually start to ripen in August. The ripe coffee fruit is called a "cherry" and is as red as its namesake, but it's the seed or bean that interests coffee drinkers.

48   The Holualoa Kona Coffee Company: Marketing Memorable Experiences and High-Quality Products

Cherries are harvested by hand and transported to the wet mill. In the old days, they used the "Kona Nightingale" donkeys, but today, these have been replaced by tractors and trucks to do the hauling. A pulper extracts the beans which then go into a fermenting and rinsing tank to clean off the remaining flesh. Once cleaned, beans are transferred to the drying shed, spread out on a second-story wooden floor, and periodically turned to dry under solar power. Wes explained, "I prefer the old style to check dryness, which is to test the texture by biting the bean. Or nowadays we also have scientific instruments to tell us the moisture content."

"Do you see this bean?" he continued, showing us an oval, round seed instead of the normal half-moon shape. "This is called 'peaberry' and occurs when the developing coffee berry fails to split into two parts. The flavor from two beans is captured in one peaberry, so people look for it. Only about 5 percent of the crop is peaberry, so between the stronger demand and smaller supply, peaberry always commands a good price."

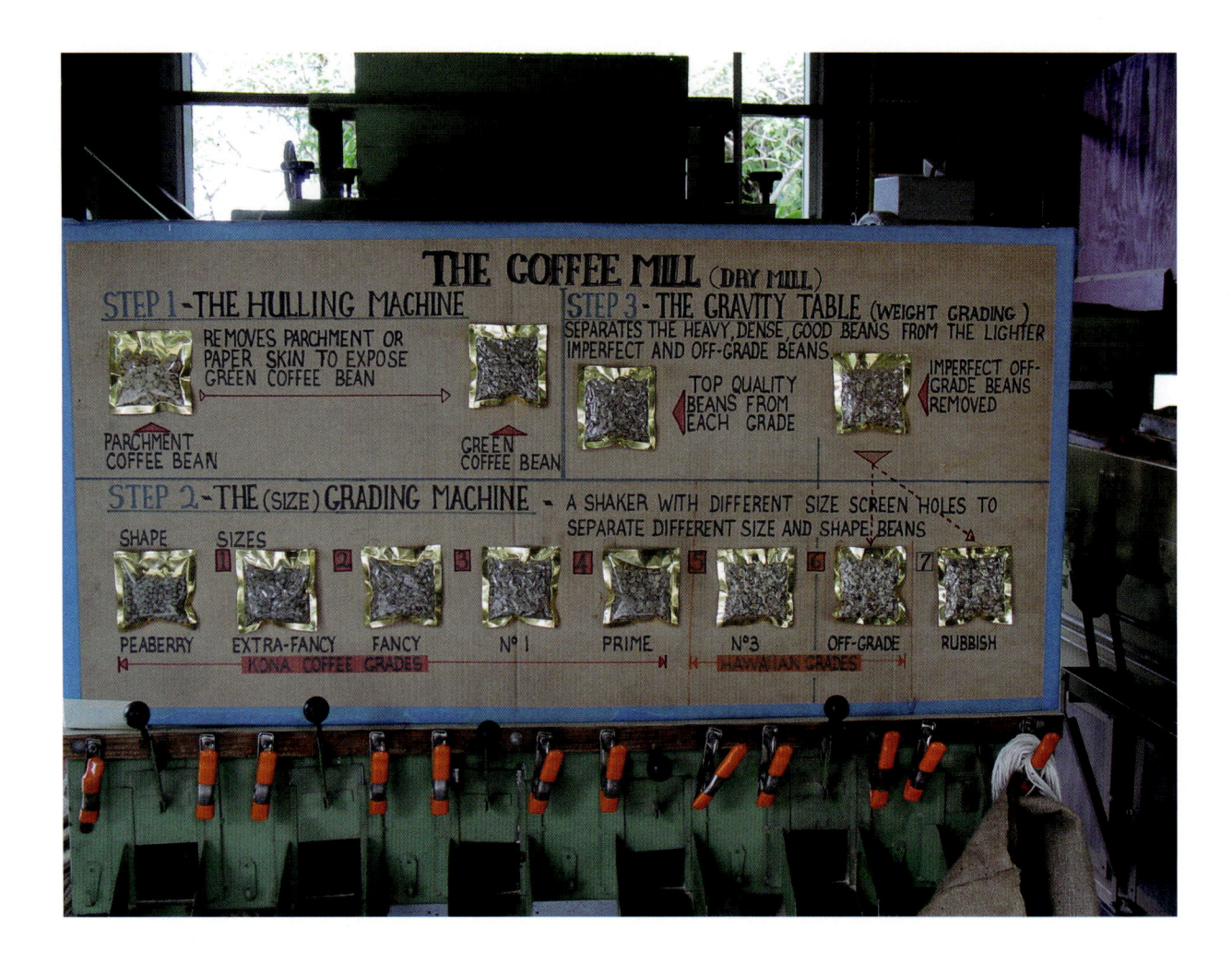

The dried bean is called "parchment coffee" because of its tan-colored, parchment-like covering. Bags of parchment are stored on the first floor until ready for further processing. The next processing step, over at the dry mill, is to remove first the parchment husk, then a thin "silver

Western Profiles of Innovative Agricultural Marketing

skin" that lies beneath. The result has a color that is aptly described by the term "green coffee," the product form of international trade. Green coffee is sorted and graded by size, weight, and processing defects according to standards defined by Hawaii state law. At Holualoa Kona Coffee Company, the beans are further roasted and packaged on-site.

Although roasting was done for the day, the delicious aroma still lingered in the air. That aroma is one of the characteristics that exemplifies Kona Coffee. While going over the steps of his art, Wes showed us the two roasters used by the firm. He explained how one is the more traditional machine that roasts beans with a hot steel drum, while the newer roaster uses superheated air. "The hot air blows the smoke right out and creates quite a cloud over the building when the

new roaster is working. Smoke gets trapped in the old roaster so the coffee roasted in there has a smokiness that many customers prefer. The result is two different coffees. We also roast to different degrees of darkness, and that also affects the final product's characteristics."

Our group then followed our noses into the packaging building where we enjoyed a complimentary cup of pure Kona Coffee while watching other employees bag freshly roasted coffee. Other visitors came in later after first exploring the gardens and perhaps tasting an apple banana.

> **"It is important to establish a customer base. "We don't charge for our tours. We earn our living when customers buy our coffee, and keep buying our coffee."**

We also browsed through the assorted coffees and coffee paraphernalia that lined the walls and were for sale. Many left with gifts and coffee country souvenirs of their experience.

It's interesting because before our first visit several years before, some of our group had declared that they "were not going to be ripped off for such expensive coffee." But in the end it was the experience they were paying for, the understanding of how difficult it was to produce this coffee all by hand. They almost had a feeling of having somehow participated in the whole process.

Story of the Business

Holualoa Kona Coffee Company grows, processes, roasts, and retails its own coffee. The Twigg-Smiths describe their firm as two businesses: first, a fully integrated coffee farm (Kona Le'a Plantation) and roaster/retailer operation and second, a contract processing operation. The firm has much more processing capacity than is needed for its coffee acreage, so they will take harvests from over 100 nearby farms and individually process them, typically to either the green bean, roasted, or roasted and packaged stages.

There are hundreds of coffee farms in the Kona Coffee belt, the geographic region defined by law, whose growers can legally call their product Kona Coffee. Many sell their cherry coffee to processors or the co-op, while many others have developed "estate coffees," their own line of packaged Kona Coffee which is typically identified by the grower's or farm's name. Holualoa Kona Coffee Company provides processing services to estate coffees without their own processing facilities.

While estate coffees help growers capture more of the value added to coffee cherries by processing and roasting, very few have been able to differentiate their products beyond being "another Kona Coffee," so prices are established by the market. An old-timer described the situation: "It doesn't matter whether you buy the black or the silver or the brown Cadillac/Mercedes, you get identical cars and the price is all the same." The market also seems to work well in maintaining product quality. Buyers expect and get high quality, and legal protection such as a trademarked "Kona Coffee" name and state certification of origin help to assure consumers that they get what they are paying for.

In this competitive environment, it is very difficult to compete solely on the basis of price, and buyers can be overwhelmed by the variety that is available in retail outlets throughout Kona. Yet customer loyalty—not only the initial sale, but repeat sales—are a major strength of Holualoa Kona Coffee Company. Around 80 percent of its sales are repeat business via mail order or the Internet (www.konalea.com or email hkc@aloha.net), and much of the remainder is sold through the gift shop. Their competitive edge is to provide visitors with a unique experience, and to have the facilities, personnel, and wherewithal to make it happen. For many, the opportunity to see, touch, and smell the products as they walk through the processing steps while listening to a knowledgeable guide is a memorable experience. Perhaps visitors develop "a sense of ownership" in the farm. It's "their coffee farm," the way others may feel about a winery or brewery. Out of this evolves the sense of loyalty.

In our case, this was a repeat trip for many in our group! We had originally not planned it, but then some members begged to do the tour, not just to any coffee farm but to exactly the same place they had already visited: "their coffee farm." So we all went back to Holualoa Kona Coffee Company and did the same thing all over again, walking around the farm, soaking up the ambiance, and then buying packages of coffee.

And, perhaps similar to how the aroma of fresh-baked cookies might trigger pleasant childhood memories of Mom's kitchen, or how couples might relive their honeymoons by sharing a special dish or hearing "their song," Holualoa Kona Coffee is associated with a memorable tour. So besides the physical characteristics of a gourmet coffee, enjoying this particular brand of Kona Coffee is a way to remember a special trip to Hawaii.

The Twigg-Smiths explained that the entire experience allows the visitor to understand and fully appreciate "one of the world's finest coffees from the tree to the cup as they tour the operation in a small, personalized setting." It is important for the business to establish its customer base. "That's why we don't charge for our tours, why they are free. We earn our living when customers buy our coffee, and keep buying our coffee."

Holualoa Kona Coffee Company/Kona Le'a Plantation is still growing; many coffee trees in the orchard are still young and have not reached their full production potential, so it is important for the business to continue building its clientele. It seems to be well on its way. According to company literature, it was rated "one of the best Kona Coffees" in *Hawaii: The Big Island Revealed,* it is a recommended visit in *Frommer's 2000-Hawaii,* and it was featured in *Watch It Made In the U.S.A.,* a visitor's guide to America's favorite homegrown products.

What are prominent threats? Every crop has its problems, and this one is no different as far as issues relating to weather, land, labor, chemicals, etc. A particularly serious problem affecting the entire Kona Coffee industry is the root-knot nematode, a pest that eventually kills affected plants. Fortunately, a solution exists but it is a costly one since nematode-resistant replacements are expensive, and a number of years are required for replanted orchards to mature. An infestation was discovered on Kona Le'a Plantation, just downslope of the coffee roasting building. Rather than replacing the trees with more coffee, the Twigg-Smiths chose to plant cacao. An immediate benefit was the additional diversity these plants added to the garden. For the longer term, it will be interesting to revisit the farm once the cacao trees mature and start producing cocoa pods.

The company targets visitors from the U.S. mainland and Canada as their main customer group, so the weakness of the U.S. and state economies and especially September 11th caused even more significant problems. Besides the overall drop in tourism, Holualoa especially felt the impact of reductions made by cruise lines that previously had scheduled Kailua as a regular port of call. Just one ship unloads hundreds of passengers, each of whom is a potential visitor to the farm, so bypassing Kona or canceling a cruise has a major, serious impact. Businesses everywhere are trying their best to cope with these problems and plan for the future. One possibility for Holualoa Kona Coffee Company is to pursue the Japanese visitor market. However, that involves a substantial investment in translation and market research, as well as the need to hire Japanese-speaking personnel. Japan's economic recession has also severely affected that market segment.

Is the business replicable? The capital requirements to create a similar operation would probably be prohibitive and would likely result in industry overcapacity in terms of wet and dry processing mills. Modifying one of the existing processors would entail substantial costs just to meet safety and liability issues; then a mail order and/or Internet operation would need to be developed. For Holualoa Kona Coffee Company, one bright side of the economic downturn is it makes such investments even more prohibitive. A more provocative opportunity exists in other crops where high quality is recognized and where processing or other activities would be of interest to visitors. Two crops/products gaining interest in Hawaii are chocolate and vanilla.

Key Points/Guiding Principles

Here are some inter-related principles that guide this business:

- Producing a high-quality product is a prerequisite when dealing with a high-end, high-priced product. Kona Coffee is one of the world's finest coffees, and Holualoa Kona Coffee strives to be among the best of the best.

- Build on the maxim: "It is easier to keep an existing customer than to create a new one." To it add: "Make it easy to be a new customer."

- With so many competing estate coffees, farm tours have proven to be a successful method for Holualoa Kona Coffee Company to differentiate its product and make it stand out from the competition's. The tours serve two purposes: they enhance customers' memories of a Hawaiian vacation, and they help equate Holualoa Kona Coffee Company's product with "Kona Coffee."

- Take a longer-run perspective. Holualoa Kona Coffee Company uses the farm tour not as an end in itself, but as a way to build their customer base and consumer loyalty.

- While it is true that Holualoa Kona Coffee Company is producing and selling a high-quality product, they are also re-selling the experience of being on the farm and observing the creation of this high-quality product.

Contact Information

Desmond and Lisen Twigg-Smith
Holualoa Kona Coffee Company
Kona Le`a Plantation
77-6261 Mamalahoa Hwy
Holualoa, HI 96725

808-322-9937
hkc@aloha.net
www.konalea.com

Stuart T. Nakamoto
Department of Human Nutrition, Food, and
   Animal Sciences (UH-HNFAS)
University of Hawaii
1955 East-West Road, AgSci 314B
Honolulu, HI 96822
808.956.8125
snakamo@hawaii.edu

Kent Fleming
Department of Tropical Plant and Soil
   Sciences (UH-TPSS)
University of Hawaii
Kona Extension Office
PO Box 208
Kealakekua, HI 96750
808.322.9136
fleming@hawaii.edu

Sunfresh Farms

A Project That Quickly Mushroomed into a Large Direct-Marketing Business

Russell Tronstad

In 1991, Kathleen Duncan was working as an early education consultant for the state of Arizona, while her husband, Arnott, was farming full time, growing vegetables on 2,000 acres of land that had been in his family for four generations. Kathleen wanted to spend more time at home with their two sons who were three and one at the time. She also saw a great need in her job to educate children on the origination of food. The husband and wife team decided to "marry" their occupations of farming and early childhood education by hosting school bus tours on their farm.

The Evolution of a Direct-Marketing Enterprise
Kathleen originally planned to return to her career after their kids were in school, but that was before she realized that this "project" would grow faster than they ever imagined. For the first year of school bus tours, Arnott and Kathleen did not hire any extra help and they took turns at hosting each bus tour as it went around the farm. Demand for their school bus tours spread quite rapidly. Eventually they hired staff and opened up their farm to most of the schools in the valley. In their first year of bringing the public to their farm, they had over 20,000 school children tour their operation. At the same time, they found themselves venturing into other activities and profit centers in order to meet their consumers' requests. For example, after students had visited their farm as part of a school tour, their families would sometimes call wanting to have a birthday party at Sunfresh Farms. Soon the Duncans expanded their farm business to include private parties for birthdays, company parties, and celebrations for other special events.

The first year Sunfresh Farms was open to the public, they hosted a weekend pumpkin festival in addition to their school bus tours. The pumpkin festival was a big hit so they expanded it into a three-weekend event. The Duncans have also tried sweet corn, melon, and Christmas festivals, but have had limited success with these events. To address consumers' requests for fresh and pesticide-free produce, they developed 20 acres of organic U-pick. They also started supplying produce to a restaurant located only a few miles from their farm. After they had been

> **"Focus on a few things and do them well rather than try to do everything to please everybody."**

in direct marketing for about four years, they also added a retail bakery and farmers' market. The bakery was open on weekends and offered consumers a year-round reason for going to their farm.

Selecting Profit Centers

While the Duncans quickly developed many different activities or profit centers on their farm, they also felt a need to become more focused. In the summer of 2000, they made a very conscious decision to scale back on the number of activities they would offer. As Kathleen expressed it: "We realized a need to focus on a few things and do them well rather than try to do everything to please everybody." Some consumers would want them open at 6:00 A.M. while others preferred them to be open late and to have their farmers' market open every day of the year. In addition, some customers wanted them to deliver fresh baked goods to their doorstep while others would rather buy retail goods from their local supermarket. When the Duncans selected their profit centers, two criteria or questions were asked: (1) how financially sustainable or profitable was the activity, and (2) how emotionally rewarding was the activity or event?

Initially, the Duncans were having difficulty tracking and separating the profitability of the direct-marketing component from the commercial farm. Two years ago they split the two entities from a legal and accounting perspective and began to track the expenses, overhead, and revenues that were associated with the different direct-marketing activities on their farm. Because their employees could switch from one event to another on the same day and common physical resources such as equipment and buildings were being used for multiple activities, they felt that they needed to get a better handle on their actual costs for pricing and business planning. To accomplish this, they utilized a computer record-keeping program and placed multiple categories on each employee's time card to precisely account for the expenses associated with each activity. For example, if an employee was driving a tractor in a vegetable field for the first four hours of the morning, then worked as host for a school bus tour for one hour, and subsequently moved to work on the parking lot for the upcoming weekend pumpkin festival for the next three and one half hours—the employee's time card would record specific times for the commercial farm (4 hours), school tours (1 hour), and pumpkin festival (3.5 hours). Tracking at this level of detail for their labor was crucial for them to better understand the profitability of each direct-marketing activity. In addition, this detailed level of expense tracking helped them in setting prices for their different events.

In evaluating the financial profitability and emotional reward of all their different direct-marketing activities, they narrowed their focus down to three activities: school tours, their three-weekend pumpkin festival, and scheduled private parties. The Duncans do not view the school tours as something that they are ever going to get rich at, but they do cover their costs and the school tours are the most satisfying activity. As in their beginning, educating school children about agriculture is their passion. School tours also provide justification for keeping "overhead items" such as their petting zoo, earthworm tunnel, living history barn, antique tractor display, and covered picnic areas that customers use during their pumpkin festival, which has the potential to generate significant revenue for them. The school tours also allow them to keep several employees on a year-round basis and the income from the school tours is very stable. The year 2000 was a "crop failure" year for the Phoenix area pumpkin festivals since two out of the four weekends in October were "rained out." Special events are another profit center they selected to focus on because they complement the labor and resource requirements of the school tours and pumpkin festival.

U-pick is an activity that they found very rewarding to have on their farm. Kathleen says, "U-pick allows people to see firsthand how production and harvesting occur on the farm and we receive great satisfaction giving individuals this experience." However, the bottom line of the U-pick did not pencil out financially for them, so they no longer offer U-pick. They also sold organic produce to a five star-resort a few miles down the road from their farm. The "value-added" associated with this activity was generally viewed as high, but the logistics of seasonal production and the service demands of the chefs proved to be too great for them to overcome. Their retail bakery and farmers' market are other activities that they no longer provide. Having the bakery open every weekend was a commitment that tied them down, wore them out, and they did not receive any special satisfaction from either of these enterprises.

The weather can be quite warm when it is time for the melon and sweet corn festivals, so these events never attracted huge numbers of people. Pumpkin festival season comes when the weather is generally very mild, autumn is in the air, and families are looking for activities that they can do together outside. The pleasant atmosphere of the fall season makes the pumpkin festival more rewarding for Sunfresh Farms and also helps draw very large crowds. They have around

40,000 people attend their three-weekend event, and it continues to grow. On one day during the festival, over 9,000 people came to the farm. Although they felt that their Christmas festival had numerous, fun activities and great weather, very few people attended. People tend to be so occupied with Christmas parties, shopping for gifts, and other Christmas-related activities that it is difficult to get families out to the farm between Thanksgiving and Christmas.

Market Research

Sunfresh Farms has never hired anyone to conduct market surveys of their customer base or to do formal market research, but they have utilized several informal market research tools to help them in making their business decisions. Kathleen says, "Listening to the customer firsthand has been our best market research." Because Sunfresh Farms is located on one site, and because all of their customers pass through their entrance gates, the Duncans believe having an open ear to complaints and compliments allows them to see how they can continually improve their farm experience. It is important to realize, however, that you cannot be everything to everyone if you are using firsthand customer feedback for market research.

To gain additional market research, the Duncans have also gone to several of the farm trade shows in order to pick up on different consumer trends and ideas that they might not otherwise hear. In addition, all of the teachers that come on a school bus tour receive an evaluation form that they are asked to fill out. These questionnaires allow the Duncans to get a feel for the kind of distribution and the range of responses they might expect to receive from the general public. While hosting special parties, the Duncans get immediate feedback, which is valuable for them to see what attractions and activities groups prefer.

> "Listening to the customer firsthand has been our best market research."

Competitive Advantages

Although Sunfresh Farms is located only 20 miles from a metro population of over three million people, the Duncans view being away from a busy intersection as more of an asset than a hindrance for their direct-marketing operation. They are promoting their place as a real farm with a unique history where families can escape from the busy pace of the city. If Sunfresh Farms were not a fourth-generation farm with such a rich past, the Duncans believe that they would not have been as successful—especially when it comes to attracting media coverage. They commonly receive over two hours of free TV coverage every year. Kathleen attributes most of this media attention to the fact that they have a real farm with a real story and an extensive history that sets them apart from their competition. "We are not a Disney-created experience, and if we were, I doubt that our business would have ever taken off."

The Duncans realized early on that their competition was neither the supermarket nor other places that sell produce, but businesses that sell family entertainment. Places such as the Phoenix Zoo, pizza restaurants with stages, and movie theatres are their main competitors. Education is the primary tool they prefer to use in order to differentiate themselves from their competitors. For example, a wagon ride during their pumpkin festival is more than just a journey across the farm; the ride passes by a collection of old and new plows and farming implements, thus providing a historical perspective on farming.

School tours are also distinctive because students are exposed to both the direct-marketing and commercial side of Sunfresh Farms. Each bus tour generally finishes with a stop to watch the commercial crew harvesting vegetables. Students get the opportunity to see broccoli growing at several different stages, from seedling to harvest, and also to see how the broccoli is harvested and transported to the cooling shed where it will make its next leg to the supermarket. Students receive a piece of produce directly from the field that they can take home to eat.

Business Threats

A high-density housing project that has crept outwards from Phoenix is visible from Sunfresh Farms and they view this as a mixed blessing. As Kathleen notes, "A larger nearby population gives us a better consumer market to draw from, but it also takes away from part of the experience we are trying to create." Getting away from the city is something the Duncans hope to preserve on the direct-marketing side of their farm, even with urban encroachment. When asked what their farm might look like in the next 10 years, Kathleen says, "The direct-marketing side of our operation is likely to be bigger and we may also find it beneficial to sell off some of our commercial vegetable

> "Today there is no such thing as just an accident—the question is always who was at fault."

acreage." Development comes with higher land prices, making it harder to justify farming commercial vegetables. Year-round production is becoming increasingly important in the wholesale vegetable industry and they do not have this capacity on their farm. They may grow for a corporation such as Del Monte or Dole for a particular window, but they do not see themselves as ever expanding internationally since they would need to supply wholesale vegetables on a year-round basis.

Managing Risks

Many individuals ask the Duncans how they can afford the liability insurance and risk for their farm when they are open to the general public. "Today there is no such thing as just an accident—the question is always who was at fault," notes Kathleen. However, the Duncans' insurance agent continues to tell them they should worry about the commercial side of their farm more than their direct-marketing component. The accidents their insurance agent anticipates on the direct-marketing side of their farm would be an incident such as someone being bit by one of the farm animals or someone falling and breaking an arm. However, on the commercial side, they have big trucks going down the highway and heavy equipment operating in the fields, which their insurance agent views as much more risky.

They have never had a serious accident on the direct-marketing side of their farm and they attribute this success to careful prevention and planning. For example, they have put solid railings on foot bridges that cross irrigation ditches. At their pumpkin festival, they hire several off-duty police officers and have a first-aid station on site that is attended by trained medical staff. They also feel most vulnerable to an accident when they are open to the general public instead of the school bus tours and private parties. "With the school tours we know exactly how many students and chaperones are coming," notes Kathleen. They also have a good idea of how many people will be coming for any private scheduled parties. Knowing in advance how many people will be on their farm allows them to better anticipate the number of supervisory staff they will need. Matching appropriate staff numbers to the number of people on their farm at any given moment is key to feeling that they have control of any potential accidents that may occur.

Another risk the Duncans face in their direct-marketing business is weather. As noted earlier, October of 2000 was an exceptionally wet month; due to the rain, the Duncans and several direct marketers deemed their pumpkin festivals as crop failures. A rained out company party means that the Duncans will not have to irrigate the commercial side of their farm, but rarely does the weather cooperate so that both sides of their operation benefit. Because of continual weather risks, the Duncans looked into special event insurance to cover the risk of being rained out one of the days of their three-weekend pumpkin festival. This insurance does not cover the event if it has rained the day before and people cannot get to the farm because of flooding. However, the cost of this insurance was too high for the level of coverage they would receive compared to their overall risk exposure from rain. Kathleen says, "If the pumpkin festival continues to grow and more dollars are at stake, we will probably revisit special event insurance to ensure the financial viability of our farm."

Guiding Principles Gleaned

In looking back at the business evolution and decisions made by Sunfresh Farms, some key points come to the surface.

- It is not a sustainable business model to try and be all things to all consumers, especially when starting out. Sooner or later the business needs to focus on doing a few things well rather than trying to do everything in an attempt to appease everyone.

- Detailed records on Sunfresh Farm's labor and overhead costs were necessary to get a handle on the profitability of each of the Duncans' direct-marketing events and activities. These records were helpful for pricing and determining the specific events and activities to focus on or to eliminate. In addition to financial profitability, the "emotional satisfaction" the Duncans received from different events was used to help select what profit centers they would eliminate or keep.

- Sunfresh Farms is a fourth-generation owned farm with a rich history. This separates their customers' experience from other competing, family entertainment businesses. Children on their school bus tours have a one-of-a-kind experience, getting to see both the direct-marketing and the commercial side of Sunfresh's 2,000 acres.

- Their insurance agent views the risks associated with the commercial side of their farm as being much greater than the direct-marketing component of their operation. They have never had a serious accident on the direct-marketing side of their farm and they attribute this to careful preparation and planning for the worst.

Risk Assessment Update

Since the interview for this article, the risks associated with hosting festivals and school tours have taken on new meaning for the Duncans. Luke Air Force Base is not far from the site where the Duncans hold their festivals and school bus tours. Their direct-marketing site is below the flight path of military jets landing and taking off from this base. Recently, their location was deemed a potential safety hazard for the public since these jets often carry live bombs. A state law was passed in 2001 to restrict development in what has been called the "accident potential zone" of Luke Air Force Base. Due to this safety risk, the Duncans have been forced to close down their school bus tours and they held a limited festival in fall 2002. The future of their direct-marketing operation is very uncertain at this point. Some talk has been made of relocating their facilities to a different site that is not in the immediate flight path of the jets, but nothing concrete has happened and this would be quite costly. Commercial agriculture may be the future for most of the Duncans' farmland that lies in the immediate flight path of the military training jets.

Contact Information

Kathleen and Arnott Duncan
17203 W. Indian School Road
Goodyear, AZ 85338

623.853.9880
www.duncanfamilyfarms.com

Russell Tronstad
Department of Agricultural and Resource Economics
Economics Building, Room 434
University of Arizona
Tucson, AZ 85721-0023

520.621.2425
tronstad@ag.arizona.edu

English Farm

Krazy Korn Maze

Rod Sharp

Bill and Kathy English live in western Colorado where they have grown sweet corn, vegetables, pumpkins, and squash on their 120-acre farm. They farm in a rural county with a total population of 28,000 people. An additional 150,000 people live in the surrounding counties. After seeing a corn maze in eastern Colorado, they decided to build and offer a maze to the schools and communities in their region.

There were several reasons Bill and Kathy liked the idea of developing a maze on their farm. They already had pumpkin patches and scarecrows that area children visited. The maze was a nice complement to their existing activities. It provided an opportunity to educate school children about agriculture. It provided a fun activity for families throughout the western slope of Colorado and eastern Utah. And finally, it provided an alternative source of income for the farm.

Before developing the maze, Bill and Kathy would attract 2,000 to 4,000 people to their roadside fruit and vegetable stand and pumpkin patches each year. More than ten thousand people visited their farm the first year of the maze. They worked hard to provide for a variety of different visitors. They offered a hay bale maze for their younger guests (under six years old) and they designed a section of the maze that would accommodate wheel chairs. The maze attracted visitors from up to 150 miles away.

Threats to the Business

Currently, Bill and Kathy have the only corn maze in western Colorado. The biggest threat to their business is the potential competition from other farmers in their geographic area. More corn mazes in the area would spread out the people that visit them, resulting in fewer people visiting each individual maze. Since most of the cost of developing a corn maze is the design and cutout of the maze, fewer visitors would significantly reduce profits.

Inviting the public to the farm is also a risk to the business. Exorbitant premiums for liability insurance coverage could prevent the Englishes from doing the maze. To date, Bill and Kathy have been able to add on an affordable $1,000,000 liability insurance policy from September 15 through October 31.

Product Pricing
Determining the price to experience the maze was based on what other mazes in other areas were charging and on the specific costs the Englishes incurred in physically producing the maze. The design and cutout alone runs them about $300 per acre. Since the communities in western Colorado are not wealthy, Bill and Kathy decided to price their product at the lower end of the scale to make it affordable for school kids and families in the community. Delta County is one of the poorest counties in Colorado with high unemployment and low per capita income.

Competitive Edge
There are several reasons why the Englishes have a competitive edge. Currently, there are no local competitors to share in their market. The closest maze is in eastern Colorado and provides no direct competition.

Another advantage for Bill and Kathy is their experience. Developing a maze is not simple, and it is hard work. They know how to do a maze and have the local contacts necessary for designing and developing one. In 2001, their maze was shaped like the Colorado state flag. In 2002, they did a maze based on the "Wizard of Oz." By changing their maze design, each year is a new experience for their customers.

Both Bill and Kathy have outgoing personalities and really enjoy working with kids. These qualities are very important when dealing with the public.

> **By changing their maze design, each year is a new experience for their customers.**

Future Changes

No major changes are expected for the future. However, Bill and Kathy would like to improve on the quality and complexity of the maze. They feel it is important to continually change and improve to remain competitive.

Guiding Principles

- To stay competitive, you may need to update your products or services on an annual basis, particularly if you are providing entertainment to the public.

- Your customer base may have a strong connection to your pricing policy. Consider who you actually market to or want to market to when you set your prices.

Contact Information

Kathy and Bill English
52110 Amber Road
Delta, CO 81416

970.874.5629

Rod Sharp
Colorado State University
Cooperative Extension
2764 Compass Dr., Suite 232
Grand Junction, CO 81506

970.245.9149
rsharp@coop.ext.colostate.edu

Schnepf Farms

The Southwest's Premier Family Entertainment Farm

Russell Tronstad

Schnepf Farms celebrated their 60th anniversary not long ago, but they only recently switched from commercial farming to direct marketing and entertainment. Schnepf Farms is located in Queen Creek, Arizona, about 50 miles southeast of Phoenix.

From 1941 until the late 1970s, the Schnepf family's livelihood came from commercial potato and cotton production. In the mid-1970s, they realized those commodities would not sustain future generations. At the same time, Ray Schnepf started a large vegetable garden, mostly as a hobby, but it produced so much that he began selling fresh vegetables to the public. In the 1980s, Schnepf Farms added a country store as a retail outlet for their fresh vegetables and tree fruit. By the early 1990s, it was clear that, if they wanted to stay in farming, they needed to market more crops directly to the public. So, they expanded their country store and vegetable garden area.

Ray's son, Mark, a fourth-generation farmer, currently operates the direct-marketing and entertainment side of Schnepf Farms with his wife, Carrie. To draw more people to the farm and country store, the Schnepfs added festivals. Their goal is to provide quality, family entertainment in a safe farm setting, while educating visitors about Arizona's agriculture.

In 1993, Schnepf Farms hosted its first Spring Peach Festival, and in 1996, its first Pumpkin and Chili Festival, which became their most profitable event. The festival runs Thursday through Sunday for four consecutive weekends in October and attracts 30,000 to 40,000 visitors. In recent years, they've added train rides, comedy acts, carousel rides, a 20-foot high Witch Mountain slide, hayrides, a corn maze, blacksmith shop, and other attractions. They also lease 250 acres of their farm for other large events such as the country-western music festival, Country Thunder USA, which hosted over 150,000 people over four days in 1999. Campground facilities offering dry, partial, or full RV hookups from October through March, company parties, and school bus tours round out the farm's direct-market offerings.

Selecting Profit Centers

The Schnepfs have experienced failures, as well as successes, introducing new activities. Their primary goal of creating positive, memorable experiences for families offers emotional, if not always financial, rewards. Still, they feel that if they create the right experience for families, it will eventually be a financial success.

Because the Schnepfs track revenue from each activity (rides, pumpkin patch, dinners, ice cream shop, vending machines, etc.), they know what people are willing to spend money on. They also track costs just as closely to quantify their returns. However, they realize they cannot accurately measure stand-alone activities since a visit to their farm is a package event. For example, they don't expect the craft activities in the kids' barn during their Pumpkin and Chili Party to ever show a net profit. "The kids' barn is always a net loss by itself, but people love it so much that it draws them to our farm," Mark said. Thus, the complementarity of activities and events is what makes their operation profitable.

Although Schnepf Farms' direct marketing started in the garden, that area is not profitable. However, they view it as essential to their operation because it is a crucial part of the experience they want to create. "Providing the opportunity for children and families to experience harvesting produce is a large part of our mission and what Schnepf Farms is all about," Mark says. It has provided production and marketing challenges, though. In 1997, they converted their garden from conventional to organic production, partly in response to consumer concerns about pesticides. But they ended up with so many insects and weeds that customers expressed great dissatisfaction with the cosmetic quality of their produce. Mark said they may try organic again, if they can master production techniques.

The U-Pick business from their 30-acre peach, apricot, plum, and apple orchards is more profitable than their garden, but is viewed more as a vehicle to attract people who will spend money on other activities, as well. "The agricultural experience associated with harvesting or getting one's hands dirty is something we always plan to offer, but we also want folks to stay for five to six hours when they visit our farm," Mark indicates.

Having the country store open every weekend, year-round was part of their direct-marketing roots, but it proved to be too much, both financially and personally. Besides, they didn't have enough volume to justify being open all year. Closing it for the off-season gave them back their weekends for family time.

In 1999, Schnepf Farms hosted a Christmas festival, featuring a gospel singer group from Nashville. It was a wonderful event, but few came. They don't know if people were too busy to attend or if they didn't do an adequate job of marketing, but they plan to try it again.

About 10 years ago, the Schnepfs rezoned 250 acres, built a big stage, put in restrooms, and added parking for 20,000 vehicles in order to accommodate 50,000 people a day for events by such groups as Country Thunder U.S.A., the National Helicopter Finals, Western Sheep Dog Trials, the Society for Creative Anachronism, and the National Glider Plane Association. They have struggled to work out a system where they can get a hay crop from this property too, but Mark plans to continue this part of their business since associations and promoters are always looking for safe venues to host their events.

> **Negative comments are especially helpful People will let us know when something is wrong.**

Market Research

Rather than hire outside firms, Schnepf Farms relies on comments from customers for their market research. Negative comments are especially helpful. "People will let us know when something is wrong. If the customer asks for more rest rooms, hand washing machines, or drinking fountains, we use this as a signal to make improvements in these areas," Mark says. They did allow survey groups on their farm during festivals to track demographics.

Pricing

The Schnepfs plan to invite up to 250 people who have visited the farm at least once to participate in focus groups that will indicate what customers are willing to pay for activities. They also compare their prices to what is charged at other farms, movies, and family-oriented events, such as the State Fair or Phoenix Zoo. Customers were very price conscious in the beginning, but now are more concerned about quality, experience, and education. Many are younger affluent families looking for a quality experience for their children.

Competitive Edge

The Schnepfs feel they have a competitive edge over other places combining agriculture and entertainment because they are a legitimate working farm. When asked how many other agriculture-and-entertainment farms their area could support, Mark says, "I'm a big advocate for the opportunities of entertainment farming, including our area. Currently, we have other U-Picks and specialty shops in the area that complement, rather than compete with, our business." He sees plenty of room for farms to provide experiences different from theirs. "Lots of people want to 'get back to the soil' and have a farm experience, so agricultural entertainment will likely continue to grow." Attracting customers is a challenge, so having other businesses in the area would likely draw more people.

Mark notes, however, that the personal skills needed for direct marketing are much different from those required for traditional farming. "Personality is very important for this kind of a business," he says. "You need to be very patient and like to be around large crowds. You will have people walking in all kinds of places that you don't expect them to be, and asking all kinds of questions."

Managing Risks

One of the Schnepfs' biggest risks is having someone get hurt on their farm. They worry about liability and the negative publicity an accident would create. It would be difficult to repair the damage to their image of a safe place for families. Thus, they continually look for ways to make their farm safer. They also have liability insurance since it is impossible to foresee every hazard. For example, one visitor ripped off a fingernail digging potatoes in their garden. Another year, a seven-year-old boy severely cut himself on a tree branch in their peach orchard. "Every direct-marketing operation needs good coverage and a procedure in place for dealing with any accidents that occur on the farm," Mark said. The Schnepfs train their 10 full-time employees and extra festival help on farm safety and handling accidents. They use radio communication during festivals to further monitor risky situations.

Weather is another risk, especially during major events. "As the dollars at risk become greater for an event, we may eventually purchase special event insurance for weather, but we don't feel that we are at that level yet with our festivals," Mark says. Instead, they have added rock, gravel, and bark walkways to better accommodate people after rains.

Financing and a responsible growth rate are other challenges the Schnepfs face. They prefer to finance most new activities and events themselves to avoid becoming overburdened with debt, and to see a justifiable rate of return on their investment. They choose projects wisely, knowing only responsible growth will ensure a livelihood from the farm for the next generation.

Future Plans

The 10-year plan for Schnepf Farms changes monthly, according to Mark. They will enhance their agriculture-and-entertainment theme by improving the farm's ambiance with nature trails, trees, and local historical items.

> **"Personality is very important for this kind of a business."**

Guiding Principles

- The Schnepfs have learned to be innovative and flexible. Although commercial crops sustained them for over 30 years, changes in the farm economy forced them to switch to direct marketing to keep their farm. They evolved from selling excess garden produce, to their country store, and to today's focus on family entertainment and agricultural education.

- To measure success, the Schnepfs first ask if they are creating positive experiences for families. This is emotionally rewarding, and they feel it will become financially rewarding, as well.

- The Schnepfs monitor consumer interests and develop accordingly. While early country store customers were very price conscious, today they are more concerned about quality, experience, and education. The Schnepfs believe that a competitive advantage for their operation is that they are a legitimate working farm.

- Although the Schnepfs encourage others who want to direct market agriculture and entertainment, they note that the personal skills required are much different from those found in traditional farming. You must be patient, like large crowds, and be very customer oriented.

- Personal injury risks are dealt with through prevention and liability insurance. Financial risks are minimized through careful planning, responsible growth, and self-financing of improvements. This also ensures a livelihood from the farm for the next generation.

Contact Information

Mark and Carrie Schnepf
Schnepf Farms
22601 E. Cloud Road
Queen Creek, AZ 85242

480.987.3333
schfarm@earthlink.net
www.schnepffarms.com

Russell Tronstad
Department of Agricultural and Resource Economics
Economics Building, Room 434
University of Arizona
Tucson, AZ 85721-0023

520.621.2425
tronstad@ag.arizona.edu

Mother Nature's Farm

Marketing the Farm Experience and Diverse Products

Russell Tronstad

Like many direct-marketing enterprises, the path for getting into the business of direct marketing at Mother Nature's Farm started by selling a traditional commodity with consumers the owner, Sam Kelsall, was already in contact with. In the 1970s, Sam typically sold his pigs to a large-order buyer that had a relatively good premium program. But because Sam is a lawyer, he also had a lot of contact with consumers and decided to move into marketing pigs directly to his clients by using the services of a small local butcher plant. Sam employed direct marketing to secure a higher marketing margin for his pigs for a 10-year period until his operation migrated to more crop activities.

Sam's partner, John, was the "real farmer" and every time Sam would tell his partner we should grow trees, John would say, "Trees are not the thing." Then in the late '80s a neighbor of Sam's planted several Eldarica pine trees that took three years to reach a marketable size. His neighbor grew 1,000 trees to the acre and sold them in the ground for $40 apiece. Given the revenue potential of $40,000/acre after three years, Sam and John decided to try a new venture that they called Mother Nature's Christmas Tree Farm. Sam would provide the seedlings and technical production expertise (shearing, etc.) while John did the irrigating and cultivating. The first year they bought bareroot Eldarica pine seedlings from Oregon. Out of the 5,000 they planted, 4,000 died. Rather than plant bareroot the second year, they grew seedlings from seed in a root trainer—which is essentially a deep pot—and lost them to weeds. The third year, they recognized that they had to cultivate more intensely while the seedlings were getting started since the seedlings didn't have a canopy to shade the weeds like traditional crops of cotton and wheat do. They quickly realized that the best marketing location and plan is of no value without a crop to market.

After selling their first Eldarica pines as Christmas trees to the public, they also quickly noted the ramifications of only getting a paycheck in December. It was also about this time that Sam read an article which held to the idea that a family farm should produce year-round crops. Year-round crops were prescribed as a solution for securing adequate year-round cash flow without obtaining annual financing.

> **"A simple string tied around the corn made it worth 50¢ a stock or $5 a bundle... and fetched $10,000 for corn that was only worth $700."**

Developing Complementary Profit Centers

To generate a steadier cash flow and take advantage of the nice fall atmosphere on the farm, Sam and his family started a pumpkin festival about four years after their first Christmas tree sales. To reflect the addition of new events, they shortened their farm's name to Mother Nature's Farm. Their pumpkin festival has grown from just a few thousand dollars to over $100,000 in sales every October. Since they started pumpkins, their goal has been to double sales every year. While they realize that they can't keep doing this forever, they have come close for the last five years. Because of high summer temperatures, it is not feasible for Phoenix-grown pumpkins to be ready for the October season, so they "contract" their pumpkins to a grower in San Simon, Arizona, which is at a higher and cooler elevation. Harry Owens is their grower, but they take all the risks associated with a crop failure. That is, they buy all the inputs and Harry provides the land and labor for a fee.

Once they started in the pumpkin business, they realized that they had to be unique by offering an experience in addition to a pumpkin or Christmas tree. There are three pumpkin lots within two miles of their farm during October, and at Christmas there are four tree lots within two miles of their farm. To provide a differentiated product from the tree and pumpkin lots, they keep livestock around—goats, sheep, pigs, ducks, chickens, and a dairy calf—that the kids can have contact with. They also use a farm tractor and wagon to show the kids around the farm. A six- to eight-year-old child is their prime customer even though the farm is 46 acres with basically no fences. They also have a maze, and to better target it for this age group they use Johnson grass rather than corn. The grass is only shoulder high on an adult, so kids can see out of it and do not get scared as they sometimes do in a corn maze. Sam has noticed when he drives by the other pumpkin and Christmas tree lots on weekends that there are hardly any customers there. But the parking lot of Mother Nature's Farm is often full because he is also selling an experience.

Mother Nature's Farm is still looking for more ways to expand and smooth out their year-round income. They have tried selling sweet corn, but the heat of the summer deters customers. A Watermelon Festival in July didn't work either. Hot weather is their biggest obstacle to tackle, while cold weather is more difficult for most other regions to overcome. They are currently building a barn that will provide misters and cooling from the hot Phoenix sun. They hope customers will be attracted and comfortable enough to come and buy sweet corn, watermelon, tomatoes, and squash even during the hot summer days.

Another way Mother Nature's Farm seeks to gain a competitive edge is by selling value-added products. This includes cutting one acre of corn by hand and bundling it. Last year they did 2,000 bundles of corn in one day, which required 137 labor hours. But a simple string tied around the corn made it worth 50¢ a stock or $5 a bundle. So they took an acre of corn, added some labor and fetched $10,000 for corn that was only worth $700. Sam feels strongly that you have to believe in your product to sell it at a good price. Another product they carry is honey.

The farm used to have hives, but now they only sell honey from other producers. They carry 11 different flavors of honey, such as watermelon and mesquite. The honey is different and appealing to give as a present, so they sell it in their store.

They have also started selling Grand Canyon Sweet Onion salad dressing. The entire package is put together by someone else, and they just sell the product. Sam was surprised by the number of women that seek out unique salad dressings like this. They had many inquiries at the onion festival they sponsored in 2001, and although the dressing costs $5 while everything at the supermarket can be bought for under $4, the dressing sold because it is unique and makes a great gift.

For the past three years, they have had a gourd festival in November on the Saturday before Thanksgiving. The first time Sam grew gourds, he found that they had no pest problems, required very little maintenance, and that one gourd plant yielded 100 gourds. He sold every one for $5 apiece. However, he is currently looking for better ways to market the gourd festival. He is not sure whether folks are too busy before Christmas or whether they don't have enough word out on the event. The farm also has a craft weekend with unique crafts the weekend before Christmas. For the craft weekend they have had school groups singing and dancing, which tends to build up the camaraderie. Sam has tried an Easter egg hunt that was modestly successful, but it was quite a bit of work so they dropped it. Since most of the events depend on their family for labor, they need to evaluate which activities to focus their finite energies on.

Success for Mother Nature's Farm is mainly measured by sales since their costs are largely driven by their own labor which is rather fixed. But Sam also finds selling trees and growing pumpkins to be a lot more fun and satisfying than practicing law. He generally finds himself happier and not as emotionally drained from work on the farm, but at the end of every big event or festival, everyone on their staff is still exhausted. During events, the farm is open from 9 A.M. to 9 P.M., but if you count prep work and cleanup, they work at least 18-hour days during festivals. However, they have slack time to "recharge" when they don't have any events going on. They are considering doing an event in November, such as opening their Christmas store in early November, but they are wondering if they can stand three straight months of intense work: pumpkin sales, Christmas store, and Christmas tree sales back-to-back. For now, they will probably continue to have their gourd festival or similar event the end of November because it requires less input than the Christmas store.

Market Strategies

Sam believes that a competitive edge for their operation is location, location, and location. Their farm is situated right off of the major street of Baseline and is fairly close to the Superstition freeway, which makes them very accessible and easy to find. Mother Nature's Farm also tries to differentiate itself by being a "full service" pumpkin store. They stock almost every kind of pumpkin known to man because they feel that a full service pumpkin place brings more business in and takes more pumpkins out the door.

> "You're not selling me a pumpkin. You're selling me an experience."

They have never paid for television, newspaper, or radio advertising, but they have been able to get free publicity because they are unique. Their upcoming events are often written up as short articles by Phoenix area newspapers. They can typically get 30 seconds of television coverage without too much trouble, and they received about 12 minutes of television coverage a couple of years ago. This was the same year they had a record amount of free radio time after they received a call from a "crazy hard rock" station about their farm's 490-pound pumpkin. The radio station likes wild stunts and they wanted to drop the pumpkin in a parking lot. It turned out that this station really appeals to the 20- to 30-year age group, and these people often have young children that are 6 to 8 years old. Sam agreed to the pumpkin drop, but only if the pumpkin was dropped on his farm and not the parking lot of some shopping center. Weekend sales for the publicized stunt were three times higher than those of the previous year. Attention is not drawn to a "pumpkin patch" that's not unique. However, it is news if there is going to be a weigh-off for the largest pumpkin in Arizona and the largest pumpkin happens to be on your farm. This uniqueness has allowed them to "own" the pumpkin customer.

Mother Nature's Farm uses school tours as a market promotion strategy. School tours bring about 5,000 children to the farm every year or upwards of about 150 children per day. The first school tours they did were for free but with a contest. That is, their market strategy was to have a coloring contest so that kids would bring their parents back on the weekend with their colored Christmas tree drawing. In every case, the schoolteachers had the students color the pictures and the schoolteacher would then bring them back to the farm, so the parents were cut out of the loop. After two years of the parents being bypassed, Sam was convinced that the teachers did not understand or agree with the notion of kids getting their parents to take them back to the farm on the weekend, so he started charging for the school tours.

During the pumpkin festival, each child receives a small, 2- to 3-pound Oz pumpkin that is almost indestructible. Each pumpkin has a sticker on it that says it was found at Mother Nature's Farm with instructions on how to grow it. During Christmas, each student goes home with a small tree with a label that says, "I was grown at Mother Nature's Christmas Tree Farm."

Pricing

With respect to pricing, the name of Mother Nature's game is to figure out how much markup the farm can ask for and get people to pay. Sam has used pricing points that nurseries often follow. For example, the farm used to make compost and put it in plastic bags with the price point being $0.99. If the compost were priced at $1.29, very few customers would buy it. So a direct

> **"The greatest threat and challenge to their operation in the future will be in dealing with zoning regulations."**

farm marketer must figure out what the price point is for what they are trying to sell. Sam feels that pumpkins don't have a price point since people don't buy enough at the grocery store to know what they sell for. The price of potted Christmas trees is not that well known in the Phoenix area either.

They price their pumpkins by size. The "Jack" is $10 and the smaller pumpkins $5 and $2. These prices are so high by weight that it would be embarrassing to talk about the cost per pound. Their pumpkin sales have really been a bright star with growth for the past three years, rising from $25,000 to $55,000, and then to $100,000. Sam knows someone in Indiana that does over $1 million in pumpkin sales. Once, when a customer complained to Sam about the high price of the pumpkins (substantially more than $1 per pound) when they were selling for $0.25 per pound at the store, Sam told him, "Try taking a hay ride down the supermarket aisle." The customer got the point and responded, "You're not selling me a pumpkin. You're selling me an experience." Even if customers don't take the hay ride, they still get a little feel of the farm.

They charge $2 for about a 20-minute hay ride and $5 for hay rides that include a drop-off at their maze. Most customers spend about two hours if they go through the maze, so Sam feels that they are price competitive with a movie or similar entertainment activity. They run double trailers so that they can carry around 50 people per tractor. Children and parents are both charged for the hay ride. Sam has observed that most people buy their food from the grocery store with little contact to the farm, so part of what Mother Nature's is trying to do is educate and bring people "to the food."

For their Christmas trees, a tree is the same price to dig or cut. If farm staff dig the tree, the cost is $2 per foot higher than if it is cut. About 10 to 15 percent of their clientele want to dig their own tree. The farm has had their fields full of people taking two to three hours to do this because it is difficult for customers to dig a 15-gallon tree in the heavy soil. Thus, for some customers, the staff will give them a shovel, take their picture, and then farm staff will dig the tree out for them.

They charge $5 per student for school tours and they find them to be a good and steady profit center for the farm. At first they charged just the kids and let the parents and chaperones in free. But for some schools, such as charter schools that have heavy parent involvement, they would have 50 parents if they had 50 kids. This was just like having 100 kids. Currently, if there are more than a certain number of parents, additional adults are charged an entrance fee. Sam says, "In general, if people don't pay anything for it, they don't think it is worth anything."

Threats to Business

Each farm needs "event coverage" and "regular coverage" according to Sam. An insurance agent quoted Sam a price of $2,000 per day for event coverage, which would cover against being rained out and other disastrous events. Although they have canceled events due to rain, they have never carried a "weather insurance" policy. If it ever gets to the point that they can't afford to lose the dollars they have invested in an event, they may get "event coverage." Sam has a million-dollar umbrella policy that he secured through a direct-marketing association. They use normal carriers for car and health insurance.

Up until a few years ago, Mother Nature's Farm was "in the country." In 1968, they had only farm houses within three miles of their place. In the last 12 years, housing from Gilbert and Mesa has built out next to them. A subdivision was built on their east side seven to eight years ago. To keep from having problems with the neighbors, Sam wrote a letter and walked it around to all his immediate neighbors. He let them know, "I'm a farmer and we're going to be working at night in the field now and again." But in the last two years houses have been built on all sides of them. Through this transition to urbanization, Sam has noticed how the attitude of the community toward farming has changed. In 1968 as a pig farm, he was welcomed by virtually everyone. But now, several people around town view Mother Nature's Farm as a nuisance, even though they are growing lots of trees in some places and are providing some "open space." The farmland they own is relatively small at only 46 acres, but they also rent 130 acres about two miles away, giving them around 175 acres.

Sam believes that government regulation is the biggest threat to their operation. Whatever they want to do is going to take twice as much effort and cost to get it done. Sam feels as though they currently need permission from the government to do anything since they live on "the fringe." Sam also feels it will take a long time before they can possibly get back to a more "free system of land use" as well.

Road improvements have cost Mother Nature's Farm a lot of business in the past. Baseline is a major road near the farm that has had four improvements in the last five years and is supposed to be improved again. One year, sales at the farm were cut by about 50% from an improvement project a mile west of them to put in a 24-hour Wal-Mart store. The following year, sales doubled at their pumpkin festival. Some of this upswing was possibly driven by low sales in the prior year but some may also be attributed to an increase in traffic they have experienced from folks going to Wal-Mart to shop. However, Sam is not convinced that the typical Wal-Mart customer fits their consumer profile well since people shop Wal-Mart for low prices and their pumpkin farm is not "low price."

Sam is planning a great big Wisconsin-style dairy farm in the future for Mother Nature's Farm. He hopes road improvements will include left and right turn lanes in the next five years, as well as paved parking around the barn but with most parking on the grass. The barn will offer year-round labor if Mother Nature's Farm chooses to move beyond family labor.

Guiding Principles Gleaned

Key points and principles observed from Mother Nature's Farm as they transitioned from a pig farm to a direct farm marketing and entertainment place can be summarized as follows:

- *Providing Unique Experiences.* To get out of the commodity business, they had to provide a product that was unique to competitors in their area. In the case of their competing pumpkin and Christmas tree lots, providing a farm experience that includes small animals, a wagon ride, and a pumpkin weigh-off and drop have been quite effective for them in providing a competitive edge over their neighboring competition. In addition, they stock a wide selection of pumpkins and are essentially the only place in town where a live Christmas tree sitting in the ground can be bought.

- *Budgeting Family Energy Carefully.* Because most of their input cost is tied up in family labor, they largely evaluate new and alternative events on the basis of how much energy they feel they can provide to an event given the amount of energy they already have committed to their existing successful events.

- *Year-Round Events.* While their pumpkin and Christmas tree events have been quite successful to their bottom line, they are still seeking other activities in the spring and summer that will provide for more year-round cash flow and customers coming to their farm.

- *Zoning Challenges.* Because urban high density housing already borders their farm, they believe that the greatest threat and challenge to their operation in the future will be in dealing with zoning regulations. "Farming activities" that they used to do unchallenged are receiving complaints from their neighbors, even though they have made prior contact to nearby housing developments explaining the activities that occur annually on their farm.

Contact Information

Sam Kelsall
1663 E. Baseline Road
Gilbert, AZ 85233-1542

480.892.5874
wade@mothernaturesfarm.com
www.mothernaturesfarm.com

Russell Tronstad
Department of Agricultural and Resource Economics
Economics Building, Room 434
University of Arizona
Tucson, AZ 85721-0023

520.621.2425
tronstad@ag.arizona.edu

Southridge Farms

Moose Droppings for Sale

Ruby Ward, DeeVon Bailey, and Dean Miner

About ten miles south of Provo, Utah, Southridge Farms' big red barn lies just off I-15, nestled among orchards and grassy hills. Travelers responding to their inviting sign, encounter a homey store located inside the barn with an old-fashioned ice cream counter, jams, jellies, dried and fresh fruit, and fruit salsas when in season. Visitors are invited to sample products, including the fruits displayed in see-through coolers to keep them at peak quality.

Phil Rowley, owner of Southridge Farms, has worked hard over the last 15 years to create a pleasant image of his farm, providing visitors to the farm with top-quality products and friendly service that meets his consumers' interests. Samples of seasonal fresh fruit are accompanied by an explanation of the fruit's variety and its characteristics. Samples of preserved products (jams, jellies, dried fruits, etc.) are offered year-round.

Company Background

Rowley is the third generation of his family to earn a livelihood from the farm on which he was raised. His forefathers grew cherries, apples, pears, and peaches on this same farm ground. Hard times and poor product prices forced Rowley to explore new ways to market his fruits.

Tart cherries were Southridge Farms' primary crop until the bottom dropped out of the cherry market in 1986. Using a family recipe, the Rowleys began making jam to sell in local stores. During this time, Payson Fruit Growers (PFG) continued to market the bulk of Rowley's cherries, but prices became too low to sustain the family and the farm. To establish a niche market for his product, Rowley wanted to dry his cherries. PFG had dried and sugarcoated "snow cherries" a decade earlier with dismal success, so PFG was not interested when Rowley proposed the idea to them.

Convinced that a market for dried cherries existed, Rowley eventually located a dehydrating expert at the University of California at Davis who agreed to work with him. He helped Rowley build a prototype dryer that soon produced good, dried cherries. PFG was still not interested in Rowley's dried cherries, so he contracted a welder to build a belt-system dryer. The welder thought an individually quick-frozen (IQF) machine would be a good starting point, so Rowley tracked one down in Oregon and bought the machine. He and the welder rebuilt it to meet the recommendations of the dehydration expert and soon the machine was turning out great dried cherries. Once the system proved feasible and profitable, both PFG and Cherry Central, PFG's marketer, wanted to be part of the project. Today, PFG operates four of its own cherry dryers.

Interested in adding even more value to their PFG dried cherries, the Rowley family coated them with yogurt and chocolate, then packaged the covered cherries with clever labels such as "Moose Droppings." They expanded their line of jams and jellies and increased their markets.

The idea for opening a store on the farm itself—a farm market—was born after Rowley visited farm markets in the eastern United States during a time when he was desperate for new ways to sell his products because markets were declining. "When you walk the floor at night realizing you are going to lose your farm, you really start to ask what can I do to get more out of my products," he said. A farm market, he explained, is where you bring customers to your farm, rather than gathering with others at a farmers' market to attract the customers.

To upgrade his barn for the farm market he envisioned, Rowley needed to convince his banker that it would increase his profits. He began by operating out of his garage for five years to test the market and his ideas. This experimental garage market allowed him to write a sound business plan with good data to support his projections. Rowley's experience-based plan convinced the bank he was creditworthy and they have been very supportive.

Threats

Rowley considers new competition and food safety liability his greatest threats. Just one instance of a food safety problem could be devastating. The above threats are in addition to threats from weather-related elements one faces in an agriculturally based business. This enterprise is also vulnerable to the general ups and downs of the economy as any other type of business.

Risk Management

Rowley is in constant contact with customers to gauge their response to his products and to receive ideas from them. He has learned to be flexible and to make adjustments as conditions

warrant. For example, he plans to employ the Internet to develop markets, to offer mail order, and to keep in touch with customers through a newsletter. Current markets are constantly monitored and new ones developed.

Southridge carries liability insurance to combat the risk of food safety. The importance of food safety and liability insurance was brought home recently when Rowley's eyeglasses were found at the bottom of a vat of yogurt and chocolate used to coat dried cherries. His insurance company was indifferent about dumping the product or selling it and seeing what happened. Rowley chose to dump the product and asked the insurance company to help pay for his expenses. This is just one example of problems with food safety that can arise where liability insurance helps cover the cost.

To combat early frosts, Rowley purchased wind machines and is testing a frost machine. When frosts limit production, he improvises and keeps his store full with apples from Washington or other areas not hit by frost.

> **"A financial crisis can sometimes lead to innovation."**

Competitive Edge

Rowley is confident he will have an advantage over new competition because of his solid reputation and his constant interaction with customers who provide him with feedback. He is also creative and willing to try new things, such as the dried cherries and the farm market.

The type of cherry Rowley grows is sweeter than the tart cherries grown in Michigan, his biggest competition. Rowley's cherries are three to six Brix sweeter (Brix is a measure of natural sugars in fruits, according to the Brix scale), which is noticeable to consumers.

Product Pricing

To price Southridge Farms products, Rowley analyzes what it costs to produce each product and considers what competitors charge for theirs. He wants to realize a 35 to 40 percent margin on each product. Rowley prices his products at the farm market just under what is charged for them elsewhere, so customers feel they are getting a bargain when they visit his farm.

Market Research

Market research at Southridge Farms is mainly gathered through the response they receive from test samples at their country store. Their high level of customer service allows interaction with customers, as the customers taste the products. While informal, this allows the employees to get a good feel for what customers want. They also get feedback from people selling their products elsewhere.

Measuring Success

Phil Rowley quips that his biggest measure of success is whether he can sleep at night. He stresses that in order to track success, producers need to have an accurate measure of each item's cost of production as well as knowledge of each product's potential selling price. Hence, Southridge Farms utilizes numerous spreadsheets to track their production costs.

Future Plans

Rowley plans to develop an eight- to sixteen-page catalogue of products that could be mailed and distributed at other markets. The mailing list for catalogues will come from customers who visit the farm. He'd like to keep visitors involved with the farm through a newsletter and web page. Their current web page will be upgraded to increase year-round sales, instead of being used just in the fall to sell gift packages. Also, to make more efficient use of the farm year-round, they will start selling bedding plants.

Conclusions

Southridge Farms is an excellent example of how a financial crisis can sometimes lead to innovation. Years of uncertain fruit prices led Phil Rowley to look for a way to relieve dependence on general market prices for his fruit products. It is not likely that all fruit growers would be equally successful in following this pattern. However, elements of Southridge Farm's business practices, and Phil Rowley's personality, could figure in the success of any value-added agricultural business.

As an entrepreneur, Phil Rowley is forward thinking, optimistic, willing to put ideas into action, and willing to accept a certain amount of risk. The company maintains good records from which it tracks success. They constantly seek feedback from their customers and look for ways to respond to it. They also try to make the best use of their facilities through customer feedback.

Guiding Principles

- Determine each item's cost of production as well as its potential selling price.

- If you are able to show the bank a business proposal that has been thoroughly tested and that contains good data, you are more likely to get the financial backing you need.

- Longstanding markets can still change drastically. If you are willing to innovate and accept some risk, you may be able to reinvent your farm or products and thrive.

Contact Information

Phil Rowley
Southridge Farms
300 West 900 South
Santaquin, UT 84655

801.754.5511
rowleys@southridgefarms.com
www.southridgefarms.com

Ruby Ward
Department of Economics
Utah State University
3530 Old Main Hill
Logan, UT 84322-3530
435.797.2323
rward@econ.usu.edu

DeeVon Bailey
Department of Economics
Utah State University
3530 Old Main Hill
Logan, UT 84322-3530
435.797.2316
dbailey@econ.usu.edu

Dean Miner
Utah State University
Utah County Extension Office
Provo, UT 84601
801.370.8469
deanm@ext.usu.edu

Mebane Farms

Pastured Poultry

Rod Sharp

Looking for ways to increase profits with their beef business, Dave and Bonnie Mebane participated in a Cooperative Extension conference on range beef cattle. At the workshop, Joel Salatin gave a presentation on how farmers could complement their beef enterprise with pastured poultry. Intrigued, Dave arranged to visit Joel's chicken farm in Virginia and later came home enthusiastic about the possibility of developing a pasture chicken enterprise on his ranch in Montrose, Colorado.

The first year, the Mebanes raised a few chickens with good results. Day-old chicks were purchased from a hatchery in New Mexico. The new chicks were first put in a brooder (an old cow watering tub filled with shavings and heated with heat lamps). From the start, they were fed "natural" feeds containing no animal by-products, no hormones, no growth stimulants, and no antibiotics. After three weeks, the chickens were moved out to grass pastures where they were kept in 10' x 12' pens that were moved to fresh grass every day. In eight weeks, most of the birds were approximately four pounds and were ready for processing. The chickens raised this first summer were sold or given away to friends.

There are several hatcheries that sell day-old chicks (New Mexico, California, Nebraska, Iowa, etc.). Because of the genetics and adaptability to their operation, the Mebanes now buy their chicks from a hatchery in Iowa.

In year two, the Mebanes raised and processed approximately 1,000 chickens. To showcase their chicken products, they purchased a booth at the Best of the West Food Fest, an event designed to highlight western Colorado agricultural producers and value-added products. Here, consumers learned what locally grown foods were available in their region. As a result of this increased exposure and higher demand for their chickens, the Mebanes bought an automatic picker and built a licensed processing facility. To date, it is the only such facility in western Colorado.

The processing facility, including the equipment, is an expensive investment. The Mebanes recommend that anyone interested in building a processing facility do a detailed investment analysis first. There are USDA, state, and county rules and regulations that operators must comply with, adding a number of unexpected costs.

Threats to the Business

Rapid growth could have a negative effect on their business. Currently, three family members are doing all the processing. They anticipate having to hire at least two full-time employees in the near future. Attracting and hiring reliable employees will create additional management requirements and could diminish time spent maintaining the quality of their product.

Government regulation may also be a threat. The Mebanes attended a conference on grass-fed meat in Atlanta, where they met a speaker who had been a government inspector and is now direct marketing beef and chickens. She voiced concern that within ten years, government regulations will preclude direct marketing of agricultural products. Even now, new regulations are continually making it more difficult to control costs.

Pricing Products

To price their products, the Mebanes evaluate their cost of production and then add on a fair return for their labor (approximately $20 per hour). Using this method, their chickens typically cost three times more than chickens sold in the local grocery stores. Their customers have been willing to pay this premium.

Competitive Edge

The Mebanes feel they have several competitive advantages. Currently, there are no local competitors to share the pastured poultry market. The closest grass-fed chickens are several miles away and provide no direct competition. Also, the Mebanes have lived in the community for a long time and are well known and respected. Customers trust them. Montrose is located near the affluent communities of Ridgway and Telluride, with plenty of customers who demand and are willing to pay a higher price for wholesome foods.

> **The affluent communities of Ridgway and Telluride are willing to pay a higher price for wholesome foods.**

Marketing Research

The Mebane family sell their chickens primarily through two farmers' markets and directs sales at the farm. About 60 percent of their product is sold frozen at the farmers' markets. As they make sales or contacts, they invite individuals to add their name and address to a mailing list. A newsletter is sent out twice yearly, and an attractive brochure is distributed at the markets. The newsletter provides information on where, when, and what products will be available. Word of mouth from satisfied customers has been a valuable form of advertising, as well.

Changes for the Future

In the future, the Mebanes plan to sell directly to restaurants. They also plan to diversify by adding grass-fed turkeys, beef, and lamb that they will market directly to the consumer. They have raised a few turkeys and now expect to increase production. They also plan to build a smokehouse so they can add smoked turkey to their product line. Farm-fresh eggs are another product they are working on. Their goal is to have approximately 300 laying hens within a year.

Contact Information

David and Bonnie Mebane
Mebane Farms
19437 Pahgre Road
Montrose, CO 81401

970.249.1305
mebanefarms@dmea.net

Rod Sharp
Colorado State University
Cooperative Extension
2764 Compass Dr., Suite 232
Grand Junction, CO 81506

970.245.9149
rsharp@coop.ext.colostate.edu

Honeyacre Produce Company

Successfully Adapting to Change

Wendy Umberger and Dawn Thilmany

As Cindy Shoemaker, co-owner of Honeyacre Produce Company, finishes her weekly delivery to area chefs and drives towards the Wednesday Farmers' Market in Fort Collins, she notes how marketing-oriented her company has become. In a single decade, competitive pressure, production choices and market segmentation have transformed the Shoemakers' business from a traditional, commodity-producing farm, to a capital-intensive (greenhouse hydroponics), labor-intensive, direct-marketing enterprise. Although these changes have strengthened the business, Cindy cannot help but wonder where, to whom, and what products she will be marketing in the future.

Honeyacre Produce Company is an innovative operation that has evolved from a traditional family farm to a 22,000 sq. foot, greenhouse farm located in eastern Colorado. They grow and distribute premium tomatoes for consumers in the Front Range of Colorado. Their mission statement reads: "We believe that customers have the right to demand quality products, and we dedicate our efforts to fulfill that right by producing superior produce that is healthful, chemical-free, and great tasting." Honeyacre Produce is part of a larger parent company (Honeyacre Enterprises Ltd.) that also includes Shoemaker Ranch, Inc., a cow-calf operation specializing in natural, grass-fed beef. Honeyacre currently supplies premium tomatoes, European seedless cucumbers, and tri-colored peppers, all of which are vine-ripened and grown without the use of any chemicals.

History of Honeyacre Produce Company

Honeyacre Produce Company began in 1985 as a partnership between Jack, Viola, Russell, and Cindy Shoemaker. The Shoemakers first produced traditional crops such as sugar beets, wheat, corn, and cucumbers. However, during the 1970s and 1980s, the underground water table fell rapidly and water became too scarce to produce these commodities. The Shoemakers began the search for alternative farming methods and eventually identified a unique, hydroponic vegetable growing system that was available through a licensing agreement. They also signed a distributor agreement, which allowed them to market their produce within a specific Colorado territory.

This system failed to live up to its promise and the Shoemakers were able to dissolve their contract. Russell, the operating manager, began to seek alternative greenhouse growing techniques. Through trial and error, he developed the system that is presently used. Due to their distinctive growing system, Honeyacre Produce soon became a successful and profitable enterprise. Honeyacre established a reputation for producing high-quality produce, and Russell started to gain his own personal reputation as a leader in small-scale vegetable production.

Thanks to their continued success and regional reputation, Honeyacre Produce was able to double their customer base and to expand their greenhouse operation to its current 4,700-pound capacity plant in 1994. Numerous existing and potential growers visited Honeyacre in search of ideas. Tomato growers and greenhouses soon sprang up all over the country as other entrepreneurs realized the profit potential. As competition increased and profits decreased, the Shoemakers recognized the need to set their product apart from their competition's. Honeyacre decided to change to "pesticide-free" production methods and began differentiating their tomatoes by labeling each tomato to assure end consumers that their produce was "pesticide-free."

Market Research and Target Market

Honeyacre has spent several years studying the market for vine-ripened and pesticide-free produce. Their primary information about changing consumer preferences comes from reading periodicals, visiting with greenhouse suppliers, and talking to other growers. The Shoemakers say they take every opportunity to visit as many retail stores as possible, enabling them to check product prices, and quantity and quality of competing products.

Due to Honeyacre's original distributor agreement, and given the "fresh" nature of their product, the primary geographical marketing area continues to be Colorado's Front Range, a region that is growing in population as well as ethnic diversity. The primary cities included in this area are Fort Collins and Boulder. Initially, Honeyacre targeted customers with a "mid-to-upper" income range who shopped at retail and health food supermarkets. These stores had to be able to move at least 300 pounds of specialized tomatoes weekly in order to cover the fixed costs the Shoemakers incurred to secure this retail space.

After studying market trends, they found two secondary markets to target: the health conscious consumer and consumers seeking taste and versatility. These secondary markets are composed of men and women, ages 25 and above, who are employed, have some higher education, enjoy a healthy lifestyle, and are typically willing to purchase foods that they believe to be healthful and chemical-free regardless of the product price. The consumers who purchase Honeyacre produce for taste describe Honeyacre tomatoes as "comfort food because they taste like old-fashioned, homegrown produce."

Product Pricing

The Shoemakers keep very good records of all production costs; they also weigh and count all of their produce every harvest day. Pounds of production are then compared with production costs in order to calculate a break-even price.

The Shoemakers consider several things when pricing their product. They begin with the previous year's prices and then make adjustments based upon several variables: direct costs of production, market prices, retail markup, seasonal demand fluctuations, and product quality.

In order to price competitively, the Shoemakers inspect other greenhouse producers' tomato prices. They pay more attention to stable greenhouse prices that prevail in typical weeks when local outdoor production is not in season. Excessively low prices during the peak seasons and other atypical weeks are disregarded because they tend to be an indication of "dumping" (perhaps another grower had an abundance of produce, or it represents a one-time special purchase for the retailer). Thus, the price is not an indication of what the market will bear.

The Shoemakers believe that they have strong relationships with the produce managers at their retail stores, with their restaurant clients, and with their farmers' market customers. Retailers are usually willing to share their markup policy with the Shoemakers because of their positive and trusting relationship. Russ and Cindy's attention to quality control has in the past resulted in lower than average markups, resulting in relatively greater profits for Honeyacre. If Honeyacre is developing a new pricing policy for a new market, they usually begin by applying markups that they have obtained from their current customers.

All local produce must bear seasonal price fluctuations, so the Shoemakers try to get the best possible price early in the season before field-grown produce arrives at the farmers' markets. Russ and Cindy have found that at the end of the season (after frost), prices are never as good as those of the early market's. Consumers begin to look toward winter and seem to change their eating habits, turning away from fresh produce.

> **"Honeyacre tomatoes have a better flavor because they are harvested at a riper stage."**

Honeyacre moderates their product prices based on quality. The Shoemakers' commitment to quality comes through in their direct contact with end consumers and consumer education. They take every opportunity to explain their unique growing system and the benefits of chemical-free produce. Product sampling has become very important in grocery stores as well as at the farmers' markets. Positive feedback from consumers indicates their product is well worth the higher price.

Honeyacre's Competitive Edge

Initially, Honeyacre's competitive edge was their ability to provide a year-round supply of vine-ripened produce. However, in the 1990s, the greenhouse tomato industry experienced tremendous growth due to increasing demand for garden quality, vine-ripened tomatoes. Once consumers tasted a properly grown greenhouse tomato, they no longer demanded the "trucked-in" field varieties or postharvest, matured green tomatoes imported from major U.S. growing regions such as Florida and California. The greenhouse boom eventually brought large commercial greenhouses to Colorado, thereby increasing the supply of fresh tomatoes. Honeyacre believe they have been able to maintain their success and withstand the increased competition because of the tomatoes' unique flavor and the freshness of their produce.

Honeyacre tomatoes have a distinctive, *garden-fresh flavor* due to the greenhouse production process implemented by Russ. Honeyacre tomatoes have a better flavor because they are harvested at a riper stage, enabling the tomatoes time to develop a fuller flavor. Honeyacre's competition must harvest their product while it is still green in order to withstand the harsh machinery used to sort and to ship the tomatoes. Furthermore, tomatoes that are harvested green and are ripened while on the shelf tend to have a flatter flavor and a grainy texture.

The *freshness* of Honeyacre produce sets them apart from the competition as Honeyacre employees are able to deliver their tomatoes within a day of harvest. All of Honeyacre's markets are located within 200 miles of the farm. This enables them to harvest a riper tomato and to get it to the customer sooner. Tomatoes produced by Honeyacre's competitors are held in warehouses before being shipped, and in many cases, it is days before the produce arrives in stores. Honeyacre's strict quality control system insures near perfect tomatoes and allows them to guarantee their customers a longer shelf life.

The Shoemakers feel that they have achieved their competitive advantages through their individual expertise and the relatively smaller size of their operation. This smaller size allows them to pay closer attention to the quality of their produce and enables them to correct problems sooner than their competition. The attention to detail results in a superior, fresh, and high-quality product.

Prominent Threats

The primary threats that Honeyacre faces are increased competition due to increasing foreign trade in the tomato market, the movement of large-scale greenhouses into Colorado, increasing interstate commerce, and continued consolidation of retail sales and procurement. This increased competition forced Honeyacre to reduce their prices, thus reducing their profitability. To remain profitable in the already saturated and competitive tomato market, Honeyacre has begun to seek new markets and to identify alternative crops that are suitable to produce in their greenhouse environment.

One of Honeyacre's alternative crops has been the colored, sweet bell pepper. These peppers typically have not been produced in the United States and have been available only through expensive import markets. Similar to their tomatoes, Honeyacre feels they are able to compete by providing their consumers with a high-quality product. Their peppers are pesticide and chemical free, superior in color, taste, and freshness, and they do not have to travel thousands of miles to reach the consumer.

> **You must stay abreast of the changing market and continually examine what your consumers demand.**

Honeyacre has also seen an increasing demand for the seedless European cucumber and has begun to increase their production of this crop in order to meet the resurging market for this product with U.S. consumers.

While large-scale greenhouses and foreign growers have been and will continue to be Honeyacre's major competitors, the business faces yet another major obstacle in the distribution of their product. Historically, small, independent, nonchain stores have been the major end-consumer outlet for Honeyacre's produce. However, increased competition from large supermarket chains has forced many of the independent retail outlets that historically sold their produce out of business in recent years. The remaining large supermarket chains have centralized buying policies implemented to control costs—namely, purchasing only from sizeable distributors or grower-shippers that have the ability to secure them a consistent, year-round supply of produce.

Honeyacre's experience with large distributors and warehouses has not been positive. In 1998, they approached a large supermarket warehouse. The warehouse was impressed by their product and purchased Honeyacre's tomatoes for an entire season. At that point, the warehouse indicated that Honeyacre needed to produce enough vegetables to supply the entire Colorado chain or cease to be a supplier. Honeyacre felt that this was an impossible task because of their business's objectives of producing a high-quality product, their current size, the cost of increasing their operation, and their desire to closely monitor their product.

Honeyacre has begun to secure other unique markets. In the 2000 season, they investigated farmers' markets as a potential outlet. They now sell at five farmers' markets per week in the summer season (when their product tends to be more difficult to move). Additionally, as partners in the Colorado Crop to Cuisine Project, they cooperate with other farmers in the area and market their vegetables directly to restaurants along the Front Range. The Shoemakers see this as being an innovative place to sell their product as they begin to lose their other distributors. They find that chefs recognize the quality of their product, and, more importantly, chefs are able to purchase higher volumes than a typical farmers' market patron, so they represent an important customer segment. Honeyacre is contributing back to the local food system by providing leadership and administrative support to Colorado Crop to Cuisine as it grows and develops a larger customer base among Front Range chefs.

Guiding Principles Gleaned

- As a producer, you must stay abreast of the changing market and continually examine what your consumers demand. Lifestyles, changes in demographics, media reports, and research on nutrition and health all affect U.S. consumers' diets. You must adjust your production methods and the crops you produce to meet these changing consumer demands.

- Develop an understanding and awareness of your major competitors. Realize what your operation's comparative advantages are and use these to market your products.

- Competitive pricing (selling at the lowest price in the market) may not be the most profitable method of doing business. If you have a high-quality product and are able to insure the quality of the product to your consumer, you may be able to increase your profit margin. Certain consumer groups will pay for quality and may represent the loyal customer segment many companies desire.

- In order to stay in business, you must be innovative. If traditional production methods are not working, be willing to try new methods of production and explore new markets such as direct sales to restaurants and at farmers' markets.

- Maintain control of your operation's marketing strategy within the firm. Customers may request expansion or production changes based on their current market perceptions, but without long-term contracts, the firm must consider what is possible and within their ability given other strategies and objectives the firm has in place.

Contact Information

Russell and Cindy Shoemaker
Honeyacre Enterprises Ltd.
8052 Road I
Wiggins, CO 80654

970.483.5233
cindyls@concentric.net
www.honeyacre.com

Wendy Umberger
Department of Agricultural and Resource Economics
Clark Building, Room B302
Colorado State University
Fort Collins, CO 80523
970.491.7261
wumberg@lamar.colostate.edu

Dawn Thilmany
Department of Agricultural and Resource Economics
Clark Building, Room B313
Colorado State University
Fort Collins, CO 80523
970.491.7220
thilmany@lamar.colostate.edu

Marketing Alfalfa to Pets

William Riggs

In the high desert of eastern Nevada, there are few opportunities for agriculturalists. Markets for traditional products of hay and livestock are vast distances away, and the limited access to needed competitive inputs and the harsh climate of the region merely add to the hardships. It is here, in Diamond Valley, that Lisa and Reese Marshall have their family and farm. And it is here, in the desert, that the Marshalls have combined their strengths—Lisa's in agricultural business management and Reese's in farming and ranching—to run a successful business marketing hay products for pets from the hay they produce.

From the start, the Marshalls knew that they would be challenged by the limited prospects that rural Nevada has to offer. Alternative agricultural products became their focus and they watched for opportunities. In 1996, while browsing in a pet store, they noticed an off-color hay product being marketed as pet feed. Further inspection of the label proved it was none other than timothy hay, something they were already raising and marketing. They realized they could produce a similar but higher-quality product themselves, and that led to the creation of American Pet Diner, a business that supplies small packages of timothy hay to the companion pet market.

American Pet Diner promotes its goods primarily through the Internet (http://www.americanpetdiner.com), but its products are increasingly available in retail outlets, both domestic and international.

Threats to the Business

Lisa and Reese are aware of a number of threats to their business. First, there is the weather, something they cannot control and something that can easily impact the quality of their product.

Secondly, they recognize that their business is part of a limited demand, niche market that cannot withstand much competition. Large pet supply companies with abundant capital resources have noticed the potential of added profits from timothy hay and similar products and are beginning to enter the pet fiber market. Other smaller operators like the Marshalls may also see the opportunity to enter the marketplace as more and more veterinarians and feed experts educate owners about the need for higher fiber foods for their animals.

A third major threat to the Marshalls' business relates to capital. They need to evaluate expanding from their current home-based production unit with a work force of four to a larger, more complex production unit with a capacity for higher output. Such an expansion would require larger facilities and more labor. Land and facilities can be acquired, but a consistent, dependable, and trainable labor pool may be a limiting factor. Currently, the equipment they use for processing and packaging products is manually operated. There is no automated equipment and prototypes will have to be developed, tested, and put to use.

For American Pet Diner, this is the classic "chicken or egg" dilemma. They need to remain competitive in the business through expansion of production, yet the capital to fund production expansion is unavailable since production has never been proven. Furthermore, if the company grows into a corporate mode, it will need to analyze its market niche. American Pet Diner may be forced from the niche market brand name business to a manufacturing unit producing multiple branded and labeled products at the wholesale level.

Risk Management

Lisa and Reese strive to manage risk in several ways. An important part of their risk management plan includes constantly concentrating on producing and marketing only high-quality products. Products not meeting their criteria are not allowed into the marketplace in any form: no seconds, no discounted products, no off-labeling. Off-quality products are dumped or used as livestock feed.

The Marshalls also focus on diversity as a means of managing risk. Not only do they provide an array of products, but they also package those products in varying weights and volumes to fill different clients' needs. They market only under their private label so that they can develop large volume markets as well.

As an Internet-focused company, the Marshalls' American Pet Diner is set up to communicate easily with clients from all over the world. Through feedback and correspondence, and from information gleaned from the net and other sources, they strive to monitor and forecast changes in product demand. They keep an eye out for additional products that can be added into the business.

> **An Internet-focused company, American Pet Diner communicates easily with clients from all over the world.**

They are also using enterprise and partial budgeting tools to help them preplan, evaluate fiscal impacts from changes in inputs, determine potential profit centers, and derive product price. Freight costs, which can be equal to or larger than the purchase price of their products, are a concern, so practicing economies of size and scale through truck lot loads for inputs and outputs are one more aspect of their risk management.

Product Pricing

Determining product pricing has been a challenge for American Pet Diner. Because their products are for the pet market, the Marshalls feel that the main consumer wants and needs are product quality and customer service. Thus, they have focused on providing for both of these needs at a high yet reasonable price.

Competitive Edge

Lisa and Reese believe it is their active participation in all aspects of American Pet Diner that gives them a competitive edge. They control the quality of the hay from the time it is planted until the time it is marketed. Through this continuing commitment, they maintain and market only high-quality products.

Maintaining Client Satisfaction

Getting personal with their customers is part of the heart of the business. American Pet Diner has a very specialized customer base. The people who use their hay products generally are purchasing them to feed their pets or companion animals, not commercial livestock. This relationship between human and animal drives what they expect from the Marshalls' products. Many do not look on feeding an animal as much as they consider it serving their companion a meal. The want quality and they want the Marshalls to provide specific information on how to feed, what to feed, and what to expect.

Lisa and Reese must stay current and knowledgeable to meet these expectations. They do not use mail surveys or survey analysis. They feel these can be cost prohibitive, difficult, and not necessarily accurate since their client bases are expanding rapidly. Instead, they prefer to focus on a one-on-one relationship with each client. All clients, via email or phone call, are surveyed about their wants and needs.

The Marshalls are also aware of any competition. Lisa uses the Internet to track what is happening in the marketplace and to keep tabs on the competition. She also visits stores to look at and analyze packaging and design. She wants the American Pet Diner labels and packages to be cute and personal, so she uses colorful checkerboards, bright colors, and animated animals. The focus on red, white, and blue coloring to support the American part of the logo also helps sell products.

Business Sustainability, Growth, and Success

Thanks to an expanding market of pet owners increasingly educated about pet nutrition and needs, the Marshalls believe that American Pet Diner can sustain itself. However, the form of its business may change as large corporations enter the same territory and become competitors. American Pet Diner may well have to abandon its private-label market niche and market share, moving instead towards a higher production rate by producing and wholesaling multiple-labeled products. The rapid growth rate of the market insures that maintaining a status quo with production, research, and marketing will guarantee ultimate failure. American Pet Diner is sustainable only if it can stay focused and meet its capital needs.

Can American Pet Diner be replicated? Can its business formula be repeated? Certainly the growth of the Internet has fueled the expansion of the market. Similar businesses may be able to enter the marketplace and acquire market share, but this may come at the cost of others in the marketplace. New businesses may fail to gain enough market share since there is a heavy customer reliance on reputation. Still, Lisa notes, the trick is to find a niche product—not necessarily pet feed—that can be marketed over the Internet. The demand for goods and services is there.

American Pet Diner experienced a 100 percent increase in sales every year from 1997 until 2001. During 2001, however, business began to level off with only a 20 percent sales increase. The majority of new sales are now coming from large wholesale companies looking for quality and consistent suppliers. Client bases now include end-product users as well as wholesale/retail markets in the United States, Hong Kong, Singapore, and Japan.

The Future

In order to meet demands, American Pet Diner is making changes, the largest of which is a switch from hand packaging to an automated system. The new machines will move them into a new phase. And while they continue to explore the ramifications of production expansion, they will continue to focus on keeping their product line small, manageable, fresh, and fast selling.

Adding value to hay has become a dream business for Lisa and Reese Marshall. By developing and marketing pet food products via the Internet, they fulfilled family goals and objectives while keeping to an agricultural lifestyle they enjoy. While the future of their business may be challenging, it is clear that these niche marketers will continue to change with the times.

Principles

- Look beyond making a sale to the customer behind it. If you understand your customers and what motivates them, you can both make your product more appealing and enhance the buying experience. By providing more of what the customer wants, you build client loyalty and your reputation.

- Think past your current success towards the future. Conditions may change and your business may not survive if you are not prepared to change, too. As large companies move into the Marshalls' specialized feed business, American Pet Diner may reinvent itself to become a supplier for those large companies. This is a way of co-opting the competition and making it work for you.

- Consider promoting your products on the Internet. If you are producing items that can be shipped and do not need to be used locally, the Internet may be a way to expand your client base nation- or even worldwide. If your customers cannot reach you easily in person, this is a way to bring things to them.

- Examine who your customers are. If you are marketing primarily to individuals, would it be feasible to expand to selling wholesale? The Marshalls have a mix of individual pet owners buying for themselves and of store owners stocking larger quantities on their store shelves.

Contact Information

Lisa and Reese Marshall
American Pet Diner
HC 62, Box 62505
Eureka, NV 89316

775.237.5570
info@americanpetdiner.com
www.americanpetdiner.com

William Riggs
University of Nevada Cooperative Extension
PO Box 613
Eureka, NV 89316-0613

775.237.5326
riggsw@unce.unr.edu

Thompson Farms

Do Real Farmers Sell Direct?

Larry Lev

If "real men don't eat quiche," do "real farmers" sell direct? Despite impressive growth in farm-direct marketing (especially farmers' markets) over the last decade, many farmers dismiss this resurgence as a quaint practice of backyard gardeners. This case study portrays one farmer's path to the development of an innovative and profitable farm-direct marketing business.

Sitting in his farm's trailer office on the fringe of Portland, Oregon, Larry Thompson describes his business as "figuring out what our customers want and providing it to them." This simply stated objective has resulted in a remarkably complex farm operation based entirely on direct sales.

Thompson Farms produces 32 crops and sells to consumers in a variety of ways at diverse locations. Thompson's 100-acre farm provides an excellent example of a full-time farmer who has developed a thriving business through direct-market sales. The USDA National Small Farms Commission defines small farms as those with gross receipts below $250,000. Thompson easily surpasses that level and thus demonstrates that direct-marketing approaches need not be restricted to small farms. His production approach has greatly lengthened the growing season and permitted him to provide his 15 remarkably loyal employees with nine or ten months of work per year. Thompson believes that effective labor management (both on the farm and in the marketplace) is one of his greatest assets. While his location, personality, and skills have been crucial to his success, much of what Thompson has done can be copied by others.

A Bit of History

Thompson admits economic necessity drove him to direct marketing. Selling to wholesalers and processors simply was not profitable enough to stay in business. In contrast, selling direct has allowed him to set his own prices (which he could never do selling wholesale), thereby both increasing and stabilizing his income. By preserving the identity of his products and developing a loyal customer base, he has greatly reduced his risks. Direct marketing also fits Thompson's personality and the role he believes agriculture should play in society.

Thompson Farms: Do Real Farmers Sell Direct?

While the farm has been in the family for 50 years, it was a part-time operation until the mid-1980s when Thompson quit his job as a pharmaceutical representative to devote all of his time and energy to it. I first met Thompson in 1989, as part of a university group visiting his operation. The farm profile we wrote then described an 85-acre farm growing four crops (broccoli, strawberries, raspberries, and boysenberries) and splitting sales between direct-market outlets (U-pick and farm stand) and wholesale. The conclusion of that profile stated he was "…a clever marketer, but not as up-to-date on his production program as he could be."

Thinking about how Thompson should have responded to that profile leads to the classic management question: is it best to correct weaknesses or focus on strengths? Thompson's path over the last decade shows a clear choice to concentrate on strengths. He has further diversified and expanded his marketing program, and hired a marketing and labor manager and additional marketing employees. However, his production workforce is largely unchanged and he has never hired a production manager. He realizes how valuable one would be, but doesn't feel he can afford it.

Marketing as a Creative Process

Marketing is a primary driver of most successful businesses. As normal as that may seem outside of agriculture, it remains the exception rather than the norm for farmers. Over the last decade, Thompson Farms has gone from producing 4 crops to producing 32. "I know you didn't think my production program was as good as it could have been in 1989. I can only imagine what you would say now," Thompson commented. This diversification has reduced production efficiency, but it has been an acceptable cost. The benefit has been that the farm's vendor booths, farm stand, and U-pick operations have become far more attractive to customers. More customers buy from Thompson and average sales per customer have increased.

Identifying New Marketing Outlets

Interested in reducing his dependence on wholesale markets, Thompson came up with a remarkably simple, yet innovative, idea in the late 1980s. He had been a wholesale supplier to Portland-area Safeway stores and obtained their permission to set up and staff his own stands *outside* seven Safeway locations. While sales were never huge at the stands, he earned the full retail price on everything sold. The stores, in turn, profited from having an attraction that set them apart from their competitors.

While Thompson loved his Safeway stands, he knew from the start that the relationship would not last forever. At some point, the store managers would want to bring his produce back inside, under their control. Thus, from the beginning, he used his Safeway stands to expand his farm's name recognition and promote his on-farm and U-pick businesses. As a result, those sales outlets grew.

Western Profiles of Innovative Agricultural Marketing

As his Safeway relationship ended, Thompson began investigating the growing popularity of farmers' markets. He started selling in one and over time expanded to eight farmers' markets in the Portland area. A great advantage of his urban fringe location is that the furthest market is only 20 miles from the farm.

Selling in farmers' markets can be a difficult experience for many established farmers. Farmers must not only deal directly with customers, but they also have to interact with other vendors and market managers. This is not a problem for an extrovert like Thompson who enjoys interacting with people and serves on the boards of three farmers' markets. Such broad involvement can also lead to opportunity, as it did in 1997, when the neighboring town of Sandy started a farmers' market on a vacant downtown lot and recruited Larry as a vendor. After a year, the lot's owner sought to raise the rent beyond what the market could afford. Thompson stepped in and negotiated an agreement that worked for both him and the market. He rented the lot himself, using it during the week for his own farm stand and allowed the farmers' market to use the space on Saturday. This outlet has proven so valuable that he would like to construct a permanent market for himself on the site.

Staying True to His Vision

While Thompson is always looking for new opportunities, they have to fit his vision of the farm. His approach to Halloween is a good example. He does a brisk pumpkin business and brings in many school tour groups, but he doesn't get into entertainment. "When kids come to my farm, they learn something about sustainable agriculture. They understand what we are doing. But they won't see Snow White or a haunted house. That isn't what this farm is about," he says.

Key Success Factors

Thompson credits his success in farmers' markets (and other direct-marketing outlets) to the following key factors:

- He makes sure he hires personable, outgoing people who know how to interact with the public and how to sell his whole approach to farming. All of his market employees (mostly teenagers, but also a retired couple) fill out market reports that note customer comments so the farm can better meet customer needs. One result of these customer interactions is the 32 crops he now grows. As Thompson notes, "Whenever I introduce a crop, it has a ready-made clientele."

- He provides only high-quality products. "I may not have the most exotic stuff, but my quality is the best," he says. This includes tree fruits purchased from a farm

> **Our business is figuring out what our customers want and providing it to them.**

> **"Different marketing outlets complement each other rather than compete."**

- several hundred miles away and resold in Portland markets at a healthy profit. (Many farmers' markets permit a certain percentage of resale).

- Thompson has a full-time driver constantly shuttle between the farm and each farmers' market on Saturdays to restock his booths. This unique practice provides three benefits: fast-selling items can be replenished so sales aren't lost; small fruits (one of his strengths) can be stocked with just-picked products; and simply carting in fresh produce during a market draws customers. "This holds true whether the product is just out of the field or out of my storage shed," he notes.

- To maximize sales, Thompson tailors his marketing approach to each market. In the hip urban market, he plays up the environmental aspects. A few years ago, Thompson obtained certification from The Food Alliance (TFA), a Portland-based environmental label. The TFA label *"…promotes sustainable agriculture by recognizing and rewarding farmers who produce food in environmentally and socially responsible ways, and [by] educating consumers and others in the food system about the benefits of sustainable agriculture."* (http://www.thefoodalliance.org/)

- Thompson takes full advantage of farmers' markets to promote his U-pick and farm stand businesses through signs and handouts (flyers, recipes, coupons, etc.). In his experience, the different marketing outlets complement each other rather than compete. Farmers' markets now represent 40 percent of his total sales, as does his farm stand, while the remaining 20 percent comes from U-pick.

- Thompson doesn't compete based on price in any of his marketing outlets. That is, he doesn't try to maximize sales by pricing below the competition. He prices his product to earn a profit, arguing that even his U-pick customers are not particularly price conscious. They seek quality products and a farm experience, and are willing to pay a "fair" price.

The Future

While Thompson Farms is successful, Larry has not been lulled into counting on stability. As he looks to the future, he does not fear increased competition from other full-time growers who might follow his example of selling directly to local consumers. "There is plenty of room for all of us," he says.

However, competitors with very different situations do concern Thompson. He fears part-time farmers with little concern for price will woo away some of his customers. He realizes smaller-scale, weekend gardeners could eventually dominate farmers' markets. He also sees his farm stand business threatened by part-time farmers who sell at very low prices, and by pseudo-farms that look like farms but actually purchase their entire product line.

In response to both threats, Thompson is investing more in his farm stand and investigating other marketing options such as Community Supported Agriculture (CSA). He has the diversity needed to run a CSA program, but questions if Portland-area customers would support a "green" but non-organic CSA (all current Portland CSAs are certified organic). In the future, the farm will continue to focus on customer needs, providing quality products, and remaining loyal to Larry's vision of agriculture.

Guiding Principles

Looking back over this case study, Thompson's guiding principles stand out:

- *Place marketing ahead of everything else*—Thompson chooses what to produce and how to produce based on what his customers demand. Because of his loyal customer base, Thompson retains considerable control over his prices.

- *Be creative*—the Safeway and Sandy stories show a person constantly on the lookout for new markets.

- *Accept change*—Thompson recognizes that no solution will last forever and constantly searches for new opportunities.

- *Get the details right*—Thompson's business is very professional in every aspect.

- *Stay true to your vision*—Thompson has a strong sense of what will and won't work for *his* business.

Contact Information

Larry Thompson
Thompson Farms
Boring, OR

tfarms@gte.net

Larry Lev
Department of Agricultural and Resource
    Economics
Ballard Hall, Room 213
Oregon State University
Corvallis, OR 97331-3601

541.737.1417
larry.s.lev@orst.edu

Harward Farms

Sweet Corn

Ruby Ward, DeeVon Bailey, and Dean Miner

In an area known for conservative consumers, Harward Farms has prospered selling sweet corn at premium prices. They have successfully increased revenues, even while competing with "cheap" sweet corn sold in retail stores. Their success is a lesson in dedication to quality and in turning urban encroachment into an advantage for farming.

Company Background

Judd Harward's father started a small beef operation near Provo, Utah in 1945. The farm was similar to over 100 others in the county at that time, growing sugar beets and corn silage in the summer and feeding cattle during the winter. The farm seemed to hold no future for Judd, so he went to college, worked for a bank for five years, then ran his own real estate appraisal business for another twenty-five.

When his father passed away in 1986, Judd became more involved in the family farm. His two sons also wanted to farm, so to make a place for them and keep the farm profitable, they added other enterprises. The first was sweet corn. They started with two acres and sold the corn from the back of a pickup truck. Today, they plant 160 acres and sell from 18 stands, some of which are franchised. Judd says that without an intense marketing effort, they would not have been able to stay in business.

Marketing

Harward is the brand name of their sweet corn. The family owns stands that are located at strategic intersections throughout Utah County. Each stand is covered by a green awning emblazoned with the name Harward. This brand name and "packaging" is easily recognizable throughout their marketing area. Corn maturity is closely monitored to ensure that every ear provides a premium eating experience for the customer. The offer of a "baker's dozen," or 13

> **Stands on asphalt are more successful than those on gravel or dirt.**

ears for the price of 12, is used in Harward's pricing and marketing strategy as well. Plantings are staggered to stretch their marketing season out as long as possible.

Judd discourages hiring teenagers to work the stands because he feels they are not responsible enough to attract the customer base he is targeting. He wants repeat customers that will be greeted by their name. While some farmers follow very loose guidelines in setting up and running produce stands, Judd views marketing as a science and pays close attention to details, including where stands are located. He has noted, for instance, that stands on asphalt are more successful than those on gravel or dirt. Customers are more willing to stop and get out of their cars where they will not get dirty.

Sweet corn is not the only direct-marketing enterprise for Harward Farms. They also sell 80-pound bales of alfalfa in small lots or by the single bale. Judd has found the competition quite stiff in selling large quantities to dairy farms or feedlots. Instead, they advertise themselves as "Bales R Us" and sell primarily to people who own one or two horses and want just a few bales at a time. They get $15 to $25 more per ton than they would selling to dairy farmers. With over 100,000 horses in the state of Utah, Harward Farms has many potential customers for its hay. Judd admits that it is more of a headache to sell in small quantities. However, he believes the premium is worth it.

Harward Farms also has a custom spraying business that evolved from a pest problem in their sweet corn. They purchased a spray rig to control corn earworm, and since they needed it for only a short time, they started custom spraying for others. They also use it to control weeds in alfalfa during dormant periods.

Management

The Harwards divide their operation into what they call "kingdoms." The kingdoms include sweet corn, alfalfa sales, and spraying. Judd says everyone gets along best when s/he knows the enterprise(s) or business activities over which each has direct responsibility and decision-making power. Besides ensuring cooperation among family members, the divisions have helped the business grow and prosper. Judd Harward compares investments to bets and says his best bets are on himself and his own abilities. This includes his willingness to put money back into the business and to expand into new enterprises. It also allows looking at each enterprise and determining if each is profitable and if not, asking what can be done to make it so.

Threats

In an era when prices received for agricultural products are of primary concern to farmers, Judd doesn't believe price swings are an immediate threat to his business. This is true in part because he is not selling his products as commodities where he must take the price offered. By marketing his products directly to the consumer, he can ensure a stable price. He believes that the biggest threats to his sweet corn business in the next few years are competition, maintaining consistent quality, and personal failures. He sees urban sprawl as his biggest long-term threat for staying in farming. For example, the U.S. Department of Agriculture's *Agricultural Census* showed the amount of land in farms in Utah County decreased by almost 17 percent between 1992 and 1997 (2000 Utah Agricultural Statistics). The county's population grew from 263,590 in 1990 to over 368,000 in 2000, an increase of almost 40 percent (Census 2000). In the face of all this urban growth, Judd's goal is to be the last farm with 100 acres in Utah County.

Pricing Products

During the summer of 2000, Judd increased the price he charges for sweet corn by $0.50 per dozen to $3.50, while retail stores sold it for ten cents per ear, or less. That increase caused just one customer to walk away. When customers were upset and complained about the price, they were given six ears to try because the Harwards believe their corn is worth the price. Judd monitors competitors' prices, but he feels he offers a higher-quality product and aims for a particular market niche. Harward only has one variety for sale on a given day and it is priced consistently at all stands. There has been a small price break for purchasing a case (five-dozen ears), but otherwise, all ears are sold for the same price. A stand that they operate in a small town of less than 5,000 is one of their most successful stands and Judd believes this is due to how the stand caters on a personal name basis to many consumers.

Competitive Edge

Judd Harward considers his competitive edge to lie with his product and his marketing. He makes a point of telling customers where their corn comes from and how it is handled. Franchisees agree to do the same. Because of Harward's quality, Judd does not consider sweet corn sold in grocery stores for $1 per dozen to be competition. Apparently his customers agree that

> **"Consumer feedback from the stands is some of the most valuable marketing research."**

store-bought corn quality is inferior compared to the Harward product's. Franchisees sell only Harward corn, although their stands will sell a few other produce items such as melons or tomatoes. The focus of the stand is on sweet corn and the stand must be operated according to Harward guidelines, including displaying the green awning. Franchisee profits are based on the volume sold.

Marketing Research

Judd regularly exchanges information with groups growing sweet corn in other geographical areas of the United States. He also tracks urban expansion and the local economy. Judd constantly looks for ways to improve the quality of his product, as well.

Consumer feedback from the stands is some of the most valuable marketing research that Judd relies on. He closely monitors which stands do better and tries to identify what is causing these differences (including location, people, etc.) The sprayer he purchased to control the worms was motivated by this consumer feedback. Additionally, the corn is picked early in the morning every day and put immediately into trailers that then deliver the corn to stands directly. This way, the corn is only handled once and the consumer receives corn that has been picked only a few hours earlier.

Replicability

Judd feels their corn business could be replicated if tried in another urban setting. A large population base is seen as a necessary ingredient for this kind of enterprise to succeed. In this respect, urban growth has been an asset to Harward Farms rather than a detriment. Harward Farms has an established recognition of its brand name and many prime roadside locations tied up, so not just anyone could come in and successfully compete with them. However, there are many potential farm stand lots and given the distance many consumers travel to and from work, competition could surface for them in the future.

Measures of Success

Judd says he doesn't measure success by the number of dollars generated, but by the quality and yields of his product. Although quality and yield directly relate to revenue generated on the farm, it is the *focus* on quality and yield that assures sufficient revenues. Customer acceptance is another good quality measure for Judd, too. Most customers are repeat buyers. In fact, one of Harward's customers that moved to New Mexico recently drove back to Utah to buy Harward corn to freeze for winter use. Judd also notes that each of the kingdoms has to carry itself independently in order to ensure that the entire operation is profitable.

Future Plans

Judd has no immediate plans to change his business. He sees his task as continually improving his product, which will in turn enhance customer satisfaction. He is not considering organic production; he says if you have taste, quality, and wholesomeness, that is what customers want.

Conclusion

The success of Harward Farms can, in part, be attributed to Judd Harward's experience with operating his own business outside of farming and to applying business principles to the family farm. He constantly searches for ways to improve his products and better serve the needs of his customers. He has found a niche for very high-quality sweet corn and puts his efforts into maintaining and servicing it. When something works, he expands it. He views marketing in a sophisticated way and as an absolutely essential and indispensable part of his overall business plan. An impressive aspect of Harward Farms' success is that the family works well together to maintain a viable farming operation, even in an area of rapid growth and declining farmland acreage.

Judd Harward has been willing to do the homework needed to know which areas of the business are profitable and which are not. This information has allowed Harward Farms to expand into the most profitable "kingdoms" on their farm. Marketing sweet corn and alfalfa hay on a customer name basis has proven to be the most profitable enterprise.

Guiding Principles

- Keep different components of your business independent of one another. If part of what you do involves marketing a product or value-added product and another part provides a service, make sure the one aspect of the business does not rely on or support the other. Each aspect should be able to function independently. This will also help you see what works and what doesn't.

- If you will be marketing your product(s) through farm stands, give careful consideration to what you market, how you price it, and how you present yourself and your product. Not only do you want to induce customers to stop at your stand, you want them to appreciate the quality of what you're selling and to become repeat buyers.

- Marketing your products should not be an afterthought. Look on it as another part of your farm business, and research and plan for it as you would for your farm.

Contact Information

Judd Harward
1988 W. Center
Springville, UT 84663

801.489.9412

Ruby Ward
Department of Economics
Utah State University
3530 Old Main Hill
Logan, UT 84322-3530
435.797.2323
rward@econ.usu.edu

DeeVon Bailey
Department of Economics
Utah State University
3530 Old Main Hill
Logan, UT 84322-3530
435.797.2316
dbailey@econ.usu.edu

Dean Miner
Utah State University
Utah County Extension Office
Provo, UT 84601
801.370.8469
deanm@ext.usu.edu

Summary

Guiding Principles for Innovative Direct Marketing of Agricultural Products

Wendy Umberger, Larry Lev, and Russell Tronstad

The producers portrayed in this publication have all developed unique direct-marketing enterprises. Although each responded to different circumstances, some guiding marketing principles that may be helpful in developing your own direct-marketing strategy can be identified. The "5Ps" of *product, price, place, promotion,* and *people decisions* are a useful way to present the key elements of a marketing mix and they are summarized below.

Marketing Your Product(s)

- Producers who sell their product directly to the consumer must remember that the quality of their product establishes their firm's reputation. It is therefore important to produce a consistent, high-quality, and superior product.

- Because direct marketing involves selling a product directly to the consumer, direct marketers can first assess and then produce exactly what their customers demand. You must be willing to listen to your customers and be willing to adapt your product offerings as the market (consumer) changes. However, also remember that most producers cannot meet all of their consumers' needs; therefore, eventually you will have to determine your most successful products and focus on producing your most profitable products and services well.

- Developing and marketing your unique *product* is the key to profitable direct marketing. Successful marketers recognize that their products need not be restricted to traditional commodities such as fruits and vegetables, beef, or poultry. You may consider your whole operation, including the "on farm experience(s)," as the product that you are marketing as do our case studies of the pumpkin festival, corn maize, coffee sales, and Community Supported Agriculture (CSA).

Determining Your Price(s)

- Price is very important to profitability and sustainability. However, before determining price, your costs of production must be estimated. Remember, if you are unable to charge a price above all your costs, you will not be in business for long.

- The amount of competition and the quality of your product will determine how flexible you can be in your pricing. Most direct marketers sell a rather unique or "uncommon grocery store product" such as organic produce, Kona coffee, or pastured poultry. These products don't compete on price alone and the perceived consumer value of these high-end niche products is often more important than the price paid.

- Potential price levels can be determined by first investigating what similar kinds of products are priced at in different regions. These prices levels may need to be adjusted according to local competition, which may be seasonal, for your products. Most importantly, set a price that will cover all your costs and that you are satisfied with. Once you introduce a product onto the market, you may be able to change your price slightly. But it is risky to make large, unexplained price adjustments after you have introduced a product since you may lose some of your most loyal consumers.

Deciding the Appropriate Place and Time to Market Your Product(s)

- Another key to direct marketing is to provide your product to your consumers at the right place and at the right time. If you cannot reach your consumers, it is unlikely that you will have a very large market. Successful direct marketers are flexible and creative when considering methods for reaching their consumers. Farmers' markets, on-farm marketing, local restaurants, resorts and cafeterias, small retailers, and the Internet are all viable options.

- Selling a product that makes a unique gift has been an important aspect of several direct marketers.

- Marketing through several different methods may also increase your chances of success.

Promoting Your Product(s)

- Determine the best strategies and methods for promoting your product.

- If you are lucky, your product will promote itself, but this is not usually the case. You may have to be creative in advertising and promotion. Traditional mass media methods such as radio and newspaper advertisements and mass mailings may not be the most efficient and cost-effective methods of promoting your product. Other methods such as marketing through your state department of agriculture, local festivals and events such as the "Best of the West Food Fest," harvest festivals, brew fests, wine fests, tourist events, and fairs may provide you with better opportunities to showcase and to promote your products.

- As we have seen from the previous case examples, successful direct marketers tend to build strong customer loyalty by providing a quality product that is consistent and served with excellent customer service. "Word-of-mouth" advertising through your existing customers is often one of the most effective and least expensive ways to promote your product. Building this customer base requires friendly and knowledgeable employees. Additionally, you should